D0217023

The Path of Psychotherapy

Matters of the Heart

Ira David Welch

Gannon University

Brooks/Cole Publishing Company

I(T)P® An International Thomson Publishing Company

Pacific Grove • Albany • Belmont • Bonn • Boston • Cincinnati • Detroit • Johannesburg
London • Madrid • Mexico City • New York • Paris • Singapore
Tokyo • Toronto • Washington

Sponsoring Editor: *Lisa Gebo*
Editorial Assistants: *Lisa Blanton and Susan Carlson*
Marketing Representative: *Karen McQueen*
Marketing Team: *Jean Thompson, Margaret Parks, and Deanne Brown*
Production Editor: *Mary Vezilich*

Permissions Editor: *Fiorella Ljunggren*
Design Editor: *E. Kelly Shoemaker*
Art Editor: *Jennifer Mackres*
Interior and Cover Design: *Lisa Thompson*
Cover Illustration: *Jose Ortega/SIS*
Typesetting: *CompuKing*
Printing and Binding: *Malloy Lithographing, Inc.*

For more information, contact:

BROOKS/COLE PUBLISHING COMPANY
511 Forest Lodge Road
Pacific Grove, CA 93950
USA

International Thomson Publishing Europe
Berkshire House 168-173
High Holborn
London WC1V 7AA
England

Thomas Nelson Australia
102 Dodds Street
South Melbourne, 3205
Victoria, Australia

Nelson Canada
1120 Birchmount Road
Scarborough, Ontario
Canada M1K 5G4

International Thomson Editores
Seneca 53
Col. Polanco
11560 México, D. F., México

International Thomson Publishing GmbH
Königswinterer Strasse 418
53227 Bonn
Germany

International Thomson Publishing Asia
221 Henderson Road
#05-10 Henderson Building
Singapore 0315

International Thomson Publishing Japan
Hirakawacho Kyowa Building, 3F
2-2-1 Hirakawacho
Chiyoda-ku, Tokyo 102
Japan

Printed in the United States of America

10 9 8 7 6 5 4 3 2 1

Library of Congress Cataloging-in-Publication Data
Welch, I. David (Ira David), [date]
    The path of psychotherapy : matters of the heart / Ira David Welch
        p.   cm.
    Includes index.
    ISBN 0-534-34411-9
    1. Psychotherapy.   I. Title.
RC480.W378   1997
616.89'14—dc21   97-20314
                                                                            CIP

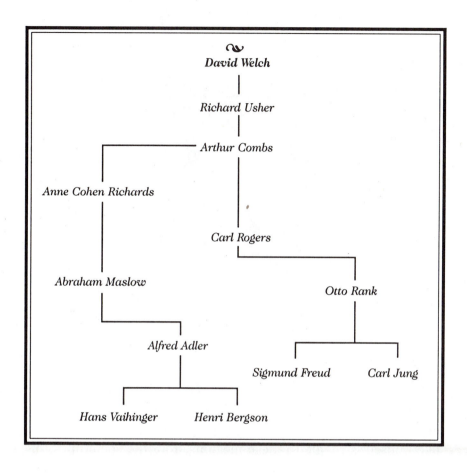

This is my family tree.
It is still growing. I anticipate that other branches will
appear but for now I dedicate this book to my teachers
who influenced me, some up close and personal and some
from a place and time far distant. I honor them and
I hope I serve their teaching well.

About the Author

DAVID WELCH is a psychologist. He is recognized as a Diplomate in Counseling Psychology by the American Board of Professional Psychology (ABPP) and a Professor at Gannon University.

His practice includes the young and the old, the well and the infirm, rich and poor—in fact, people from all walks of life who, like himself, struggle to make meaning from the sometimes (often?) puzzling mysteries of living.

Contents

∾

Contents

Contents

Contents

23

Living with Purpose   143

24

Becoming a Healer to the Self   151

Preface

∾

I live in a small town. It is a community of farmers, ranchers, cattle feeders, small business owners, teachers, and families. It is a little place in the midwest that can easily be the butt of jokes about naive hardware store owners, the farmer's daughter, and innocent basketball players.

The turmoil of the times often seems to have passed us by. The fears that are so present with many are not daily intruders in the lives of the people in my community. The strife of our cities, the battles of youth gangs in drug wars, the morality of national politicians, or the economic struggles of oils cartels come to us only on the evening news or from the headlines of the newspaper sharing space with the softball scores or listings of all-conference soccer players. Our power breakfast is more likely spent at a coffee shop than at an exclusive club. The tragedies of life reported to us on television and in the newspapers often seem distant from this, to all appearances, protected place. Some might cynically dismiss the depth of our understanding as shallow, hopelessly naive, and uninformed.

The great political economic, social, and fashion decisions are made and lived out some distance from our homes. While it is true that the rush, tumult, and wariness of the city with its constant news of exploitation, violence, drugs, and death isn't a part of our daily lives, in matters of the heart we are as sophisticated as any urbanite.

The tragedies caused by sex, drugs, death, and violence come to us as distant statistics affecting untold numbers of people whom we do not know. In the end, the tragedies of life, whether planetary, national, or familial, are individual. Statistics reduce to families and individuals and even in this somewhat sheltered place, we suffer death, divorce, rape, battering, abduction, drug abuse, child abuse, gang violence and disease. The pains of life are felt by individual human beings. They mourn death or brutality, whether by cosmic perversity or human design. The emptiness of wasted lives brings pain. The loss of faith in one another is mourned and in the felt experience of the human condition we live our lives in contact with one another. We are brokenhearted because those involved are known to us. They are our neighbors. Some part of us suffers with them.

In this interpersonal realm of life I do my work. I am a psychologist. My special task is to ponder, study, understand, and minister to the human spirit. Whether this spirit is tortured by a past of damage, tormented by disenchantment, starved by emptiness, weighted down by depression, ravaged by anxiety, or pillaged by self doubt, I do this work one person at a time. If you read my family tree in the dedication and are at all familiar with the people listed there, you know that I am deeply influenced by the theories of the humanistic psychologists. They are a group who believe in the daunting capacity of human beings to screw up their lives and in their equal capacity to unravel life's mysteries and set it straight again. This point of view places great emphasis on the quality of the relationship established between the client and the counselor. This relationship provides the foundation for the clients to find or create resolution to their life struggles. Others, of course, see the human condition in different terms and provide different explanations for human behavior. There are greater differences in theory than there are in practice, however, and we are, of course, all psychotherapists. This book describes how I work; in its contents I hope others will find stimulus for thought, guidance, and a provocation to ponder the meaning and impact of their own work.

This book is about the persons and the process of my work as a psychotherapist. It is meant to inform others, like myself, who minister to the emotional, social, and interpersonal issues, problems, and dilemmas of persons who come to us for help.

Some readers might be psychologists, social workers, clergy, counselors, or marriage and family therapists. Others may be case workers or human service workers in any number of occupations that endeavor to provide help and support for people in trouble. Whatever the title, we are committed to helping those who ask our assistance in finding their way, discovering their strength, developing solutions, and creating meaning where there may have been little. My good wishes go with you all as we walk this path together.

No book such as this comes to press without the contributions of many people. Mostly, I appreciate the careful reading and suggestions made by my colleagues Richard Usher, Fred Richards, Anne Cohen Richards, Don Medeiros, George Tate, and Ann Rader-Tate. I appreciate their help with the book, but more important, I cherish their friendship and love. I also appreciate the helpful reading and comments of two other colleagues, especially in the area of diversity — David Gonzalez and Carmen Braun-Williams. I prize the early reading and suggestions of the students in our doctoral seminar and I wish them well as they travel this tough and tender road of being a professional helper. Thanks to Michele Beadle, Christine Breier, Michael Furois, Mark Hald, Kathy Kravitz, Maio-Jung

Lin, Beth Lonergan, Patrick Maschka, Marty Munoz, Marty Slyter, Marilyn Sosebee, and Jonathan Williamson. I extend the same wish to two other doctoral students, John McKenzie and Nancy Schlie, who read and made suggestions as well. My thanks also go to Steve Long for his editorial help in making the manuscript more accurate and more readable. I would also like to acknowledge the helpful comments and suggestions of the book's reviewers: Mary Jo Blazek, University of Maine at Augusta; Dale Blumen, University of Rhode Island; John Bowers, Northwest Missouri State University; John A. Casey, Sonoma State University; Mary Kay Kreider, St. Louis Community College; Lenore M. Parker, California State University, Fullerton; Susan P. Robbins, University of Houston Graduate School of Social Work. Finally, I am indebted to the folks at Brooks/Cole, especially Lisa Gebo, who is just a delight, and Lisa Blanton, a friendly and patient listener, for their help and guidance throughout the process.

Some have heard me say this before: It was worth the trip.

Ira David Welch

1

The Way We Are

*P*sychotherapy is an un-American activity. As Americans, we share a cultural nature, and it is that cultural nature that makes psychotherapy unnatural for Americans. We are, of course, a rainbow nation—a spectrum of ethnicities, nationalities, and points of view (religious, political, and cultural) as diverse as the planet. And yet, anthropologists tell us that any society shares cultural assumptions, regardless of the variety of its individual members. We know as well that we must approach any generality with caution, for however true a thing may be in the general, it may certainly be wrong in the particular. Still, with proper respect for caution, let us venture into some understanding of the nature of being an American.

Any society, any culture operates on assumptions. More often than not unrecognized, these assumptions are accepted by the individual and relate to human nature, physical causality, spirituality, morality, and, for our purposes here, the origin and treatment of mental distress. In total, they form a philosophy, and Americans may be said to hold a philosophy of *objective materialism*.

In 1970, Philip Slater published a book entitled *The Pursuit of Loneliness*. The subtitle was perhaps more to the point: *American Culture at the Breaking Point*. In this book, Slater relates a fable of a man who, weary of the endless chatter of his neighbors, went into the forest to live alone in a small hut heated only by a wood-burning stove. When the winter proved to be bitterly cold, he cut down the surrounding trees for firewood. Then, the summer arrived with searing heat, and the hut, unshaded for lack of trees, became unbearably hot. The man cursed the elements. Rabbits raided the man's garden, so he tamed a fox to chase away the rabbits. When the fox ate his chickens as well, the man cursed the treachery of wild creatures. To keep garbage off the floor of the hut, the man devised a system of weights and pulleys. When the strain collapsed the roof of the hut, he cursed its poor construction. To protect his privacy, he kept a loaded gun on his lap at night and in his troubled sleep he accidentally shot off his foot. His neighbors were saddened by his misfortune, so they decided to leave him alone. The man grew increasingly lonely and cursed the indifference of his neighbors. In all this, the man saw no cause except what lay outside himself. It was because of this view, and because of his ingenuity, that he was called the American.

Embedded in this story lies some of the irony and paradox of psychotherapy in America. Some might ask why, if psychotherapy is an un-American activity, so many seem to turn to it for help. Therein lies a paradox. Americans do turn to agencies outside themselves for answers to their personally felt struggles. Yet, in psychotherapy they find a system that frequently asks them to search their experience for answers to internally felt questions. Another irony is that within the discipline of psychotherapy itself, its practitioners are no less American than those who seek their help. Psychotherapists are repeatedly drawn to fads in psychotherapy that offer "unemotional" and/or quick methods for dealing with the challenges of life.

Slater's fable reminds us that we Americans are reluctant to see our own agency in the struggles of life. We tend to believe that problems are caused by forces outside ourselves and are solved by things. When confronted with the ineffectiveness of a life pattern, we do not typically look to ourselves for the source of the dilemma. Nor do we tend to look into ourselves for its resolution. We look elsewhere. Some of us seek a strong *other* to take over our lives. Some ingest substances, natural or artificial, to correct a chemical imbalance or nutritional deficiency, real or imagined. Some might have themselves attached to machines to electrify, stimulate, or, the opposite, to stupefy the brain/body. Some might even resort to surgery. In America, we become disciples, take drugs, and torture ourselves in response to a philosophy of life that teaches us that problems lie outside the self and are solved by things.

This notion of separateness and objectivity can provide an anxiety-reducing function for a while in the way that any psychological defense does. It holds troubling emotions at bay and dulls any sharp pains that might try to intrude into our awareness. The underlying ache and the nagging discontent become familiar companions, and whatever energy is spent to maintain the defenses becomes habitual, forgotten, and temporarily, at least, unavailable for healthy life. Some, of course, find little comfort and seek another recourse. Some seek psychotherapy.

The process of psychotherapy seeks a center. It looks within— not always for the source or cause of pain, but for understanding. It is a process, however winding, that ultimately causes one to ask, What can I do about my life circumstances? What agency, if any, do I play in my pain and struggles? How can I live with the circumstances of my life? For many human predicaments, there is just cause for guilt within the sufferer. A somewhat more difficult idea is that there are many human situations for which no cause for guilt exists and yet the person suffers. What is vague for many is that regardless of the source of their psychological pain and struggles, real or imagined, some form of psychological relief lies within their control. Psychotherapy begins the exploration of the vague, undiscovered world of inner resources that contains the genuine and lasting relief from psychological pain for which people are searching.

3
∽

2

The Best We Have

*I*f you are trying to hammer a nail, a crescent wrench is a poor tool—unless it is the only tool you have. Psychotherapy may be seen as a tool, however imprecise.

Psychotherapy *is* imprecise. The psychotherapist and the person struggle together to enter the chaos of living in an effort to bring order, understanding, or peace to a troubled life. It is an often messy process. Some critics would have us believe that the messiness means it doesn't work. In any case, in the rough-and-tumble experience of life, people do often lurch in unpredictable and harmful directions.

Psychotherapy is more about the mind than it is about the brain. It is about mental, attitudinal, and behavioral solutions to mainly mental—that is to say, psychological—difficulties. Psychotherapy is not about physical diseases, and this is not a book about medicine or neurology. When disease is involved, drug treatments and other remedies that involve blood, nerves, chemistry, hormones, germs, respiration, and the like are often prescribed. The role that psychotherapy can play in medical treatment is in helping the person cope with the implications of the illness. That is a mental process and well within the scope of psychotherapy. And so, we are back to banging in the nail with a wrench. As flawed as it may be, it is the best we have to offer. The process of psychotherapy may go against our cultural desire for action and seem on the surface to be a waste of time, even silly to some. Yet, day in and day out, people

5

find in psychotherapy some relief to personally experienced life problems. They take the time and talk through their difficulties.

One of the discoveries made by people who enter psychotherapy is that although the process may be about solutions, it is not about advice. The person may talk and the psychotherapist will listen. In the process, what was vague and undifferentiated to the person often becomes clear and distinct. From time to time, we read about a psychotherapist who has overstepped the bounds and become not a psychotherapist but a demagogue or a propagandist or an agent for one elixir or another. By and large, however, psychotherapists are people who are committed to the principle that psychotherapy is not so much about advice as it is about clarity.

Psychotherapy is a process of exploring what is wrong in a person's troubled life—why it is troublesome and how to do something about it. The psychotherapist creates a climate in which a person may tell his or her story, knowing that the psychotherapist will seek to understand that story without guile or judgment. The person's task is to explore, understand, and act. The psychotherapist's task is to understand, suspend judgment, and be present with courage.

All psychotherapy begins in empathy. Any psychotherapy that does not have this origin is, at best, predictably unhelpful and, at worst, harmful. Empathy is a skill. It is one of those processes that fall into the category of "easy to say, hard to do." Whereas psychotherapy may be viewed as inexact by many, it is considered by the majority of its practitioners to be a science. As with any science, it has a technical vocabulary. The term *empathy* is a part of this vocabulary. Empathy means understanding—not only the words another speaks, but the personal meanings attached to those words. It means understanding intellectually *and* emotionally.

The dictionary may equate empathy and sympathy, but the terms are not synonymous in psychotherapy. Empathy does not mean sympathy. Sympathy means feeling, experiencing what another person feels. Medicine recognizes a phenomenon called the "sympathetic reaction" in which one person takes on the symptoms of another. A husband, for example, might feel the labor pains of his pregnant wife. In some societies, this is a common occurrence and husbands might even be sequestered during birth. In the original television series *Star Trek*, one episode was entitled "The Empath." This episode portrayed a young woman who had the ability to take on the pains and injuries of others. If someone were cut, the Empath could touch the person and the cut would disappear and reappear on the Empath. The episode was misnamed. She should have been called *the Sympath* as this is an exaggerated example of a sympathetic reaction.

In the novel, *The Shoes of the Fisherman,*[1] Jesus Christ is presented in a similar way. Christ would take on the ills of the people He cured and be exhausted at the end of a day. Overnight He would rejuvenate and begin His healing again the next morning. In another novel, this sympathetic reaction was portrayed between twin brothers. If one brother was whacked on the nose on Corsica, the other brother would bleed in Paris.

As you might imagine, sympathetic reactions in psychotherapy have proven to be unhelpful. An anxious person receives little benefit from observing anxiety in the psychotherapist. Having a psychotherapist become depressed doesn't help a depressed person. Thus, empathy and sympathy in psychotherapy are different. Sympathy means feeling or experiencing directly what another person feels; empathy, by contrast, means *understanding* what another person feels and being able to articulate that understanding to the client in such a way that the client knows the psychotherapist understands.

Similarly, empathy and identification are different. Bump someone's prized car and he or she starts kicking your car and yelling, "Well, take that! See how you feel when I kick your car!" Here, the owner has extended his or her self-identification to encompass the car. It has become a part of the person's self-picture. You didn't just bump into a car; you bumped into that individual. You dented that person. Nearly any parent understands well this process of self-extension; children are a part of the parent's self.

Identification explains what has happened when we read in the newspaper that an attorney has helped engineer the escape of an imprisoned felon whom the attorney had defended. They escaped together, crossed the border into Mexico, and were trying to make

7

their way to Argentina when they were apprehended. They now express their love for one another and spend their wedded life in correspondence, from one prison cell to another. That is identification. The attorney had lost all sense of separateness. He or she had identified. Such a reaction from a psychotherapist is obviously unhelpful to clients.

Sympathy and identification are not helpful in psychotherapy precisely because they provide no additional clarity for the person seeking help. Such reactions stall people exactly where they are in their thinking and in their emotions. They are no better off than they were before they came to the psychotherapist.

In some situations, identification and a sympathetic response can lead to vindictiveness. A few years ago there was a movie about two men who were famous on the American frontier: Wyatt Earp and Doc Holliday. It was a traditional "buddy" movie. Doc Holliday was by all accounts a mean and vicious killer. Earp was a peace officer. Between them, however, an unusually close bonding and friendship grew. In any time of trouble, they supported one another; even in what were frightening and desperate circumstances, one did not shrink from risking his life to help the other. The difficulty is that neither did anything, apparently, to dissuade the other from revenge and killing. If one gang of thugs said something insulting or challenging to the Earps, the obvious thing to do was to kill them! Naturally, the sympathetic action was to take sides and give some payback. It was a mathematical equation: one insult equals The Gunfight at the OK Corral! In modern times we exchange the Earps for the Crips or the Bloods and the OK Corral for drive-by shootings. We have the same mentality of bravely standing with a friend without considering any alternatives.

If you are like me, a part of you is troubled by this example. Part of us recognizes an inner appeal to physical bravery, loyalty, and an unquestioning willingness to stick with a friend—even in the face of danger. Let me be clear. I used this example to demonstrate that friends often do not help us clear up our thinking and emotions. Friends take sides. They sympathize. They line up with each other and provide emotional support; in so doing, however, they may leave their friends stuck in the middle in a problem.

Empathy is different. It expresses an understanding of the feelings, emotions, and meanings of the person. Not only does the psychotherapist understand the other person; he or she is able to express this understanding in a way that is intelligible and acceptable to the client.

Part of the inexactitude of psychotherapy is that it is a layered process. People may come in for one thing when it is another that is the source of their complaint. In technical parlance, what clients label as their "problem" when they first talk with a psychotherapist is called the "presenting problem." Some therapists view this as a trial balloon. There is no compelling reason for clients to trust a psychotherapist any more than they would trust any other stranger. It is safer for them to reveal some issue about which they have minimal emotional confusion as a way to find out whether the psychotherapist is trustworthy.

The most direct route to trust in psychotherapy is empathy. And as novices begin the process of becoming psychotherapists, many discover that learning the skill of empathy is also a formidable task. People come to the study of psychotherapy for a host of reasons. One of them is a sense of compassion; another is a desire to be of service. The extraordinary discovery that all must confront in their training is that neither of these qualities, alone or in concert, serves any great purpose in psychotherapy. They are good qualities. Nonetheless, they are qualities that might motivate someone into any number of callings. Medicine, the law, the ministry, and even politics can all be callings motivated by compassion.

Moreover, what psychotherapy demands from a psychotherapist is more than feeling, more than motivation. Simply to feel is not sufficient. What a psychotherapist must do is give definition to the emotions, to understand and give words to that understanding. A psychotherapist must look through muddy water and see dry land, as the poet Brother Blue (Hugh Hill)[2] would phrase it. A psychotherapist helps a person find a place, in the midst of confusion, to land and rest and examine life's perplexities. Finding such a place is no easy task; helping someone find such a place is also not easy. This understanding, while clearly perceived and understood by the psychotherapist, may be vague and misunderstood by the client. At other times, understanding may elude the psychotherapist, leaving clients where they were in the beginning.

The struggle for understanding may become an internal search for the psychotherapist. Numerous metaphors present themselves to describe this process: One tries to "blow away the fog," "dig deeper," "listen through the noise," "clarify the confusion," or "clear up the image." When the psychotherapist does plainly symbolize the experience of people, what happens? Sometimes people evidence surprise that they have communicated such an understanding to the psychotherapist. Most of the time, however, the person pauses to examine his or her thoughts, behaviors, and emotions in order to move toward a more eloquent recognition of personal actions and motivation.

What if this does not happen? One explanation is that the psychotherapist has missed, misunderstood, or mangled what the person meant. It is also possible that the psychotherapist is on target, accurate and insightful. Perhaps the person is being understood exactly and viscerally. Defenses may suddenly appear. How does a psychotherapist respond to defenses? This is discussed more deeply later on, but the short answer is this: Psychotherapists respect clients. This gets slippery, philosophical, and theoretical. It requires us to think abstractly and act concretely. The abstraction is of two sorts. First, you must think psychologically and accept the proposition that people sometimes act without knowing fully why they do what they do. Psychotherapy often deals with the idea that the motivation for behavior lies somewhere outside full awareness. Second, it requires that the psychotherapist be able to concretely demonstrate that the person is accepted and valued even while defenses are confronted and challenged.

Where does all this lead us? It means that a psychotherapist may respond respectfully to a person without agreeing or approving at all of the individual's particular acts. Being able to respond in this way becomes an exceedingly important belief and observance in psychotherapy. The client can learn that the content and pace of psychotherapy belongs to him or her and not to the psychotherapist. It means that wounds will be treated gently and healing can proceed as it should—or to shift from a medical metaphor to a psychological one, the person's life confusions will be understood with respect and the necessary changes in coping will be made at the client's pace. It means that the issue, problem, or dilemma will not be taken away and that the solutions arrived at will be personal, meaningful, and subjective. Respect means not judging the person, not moralizing, and not giving advice or presenting premature solutions. To attempt to solve problems before they are understood results in accidental help at best. Even a blind squirrel will find an acorn every now and then. It is just that such a squirrel isn't a reliable provider to help us get through the winter.

Psychotherapy is not a process of blindly rooting around, of trying this and trying that. People who come to psychotherapy do not come to be experimented on. Think about this for a moment. When one person gives another advice, the person giving the advice assumes the other person doesn't know and hasn't already tried what is recommended. This is an assumption that a psychotherapist can ill afford to make. It is judgmental. It treats people as if they are stupid. Consider another alternative: People aren't stupid; they have already tried all the obvious solutions. The very fact that the regular alternatives have not worked has led them to psychotherapy. It seems disrespectful to suggest to someone an alternative he or she has already considered, attempted, found wanting, and rejected.

Things are connected. An attitude of respect leads to empathic responding; empathic responding leads to trust. Trust leads to energetic exploration; exploration leads to personal understanding. And understanding leads to personal, optimal solutions, if they exist.

11

3

Coping Versus Curing

*T*he best treatment for a psychological disorder is psychotherapy. As simple and straightforward as this claim appears, it is fraught with difficulty and loaded with controversy. It represents a chasm deep and foreboding that looms before anyone who enters the field of psychotherapy. Over the years, a number of theories have emerged to explain human personality. Human difficulties can be complex and human behavior can have many causes. Because of this complexity, explanatory theories are sometimes mutually exclusive and frequently contradictory.

At the very center of the debates regarding the effectiveness of psychotherapy are questions about which model is most useful in treating emotional distress. One major approach is the medical model. This model is based on the assumption that emotional difficulties originate in physical causes and should be treated as illnesses. According to this model, mental illness is a disease that should be treated like any other disease. Thus, with the medical orientation, procedures such as drug therapy would be typically, and reasonably, employed. In extreme cases, electroconvulsive therapy and surgery might be medical options, although these two wax and wane in popularity and are currently not much in vogue.

Within the psychological community, objections to the medical model as applied to emotional distress are numerous. The objections are not to the medical model for treatment of physical disease but in the extension of that model to psychological difficulties. Many human difficulties may have mental origins (e.g., stress) that result in physical symptoms (e.g., diarrhea, headache). Other problems may begin in physical disease (e.g., multiple sclerosis) but result in profound emotional disturbance (e.g., depression). These, of course, call for the care of both a physician and a psychotherapist (from the medical perspective, most likely a psychiatrist). Whether anxiety, depression, reactions to traumatic events, grief, and other situational events in people's lives can properly be labeled diseases and treated with drugs is a source of great debate. The psychological side of the argument holds that the best treatment for emotional distress is psychotherapy.

Objections, however, are many sided. First, if the distress is psychological—that is to say, a mental construction—then of what use is treating the physical symptoms? There is no disease. One answer, of course, is that symptom relief is a positive goal in and of itself. An itchy rash with origins in mental stress still itches, and a salve that relieves the itch is helpful and appreciated. The shortcoming here is that if only symptom relief is provided, no lasting change or gain may be accomplished. What would be the case, however, where there are no physical symptoms that medical treatment could relieve? Of what use then is the medical treatment of symptoms? Let us use a clear example. What disease is present in grief? The pain is real; the emotions are in disarray. The pain may be felt physically, and it often is, but its origin is in the mind—no less real, no less painful, and not a disease. The same may be said of anguish over divorce or the phobic fear of snakes. These do not seem to originate in any physical disease. Thus, the argument is that they should not be treated as medical diseases but as psychological disorders. There is no argument over diseases and disorders that have both physical and psychological origins or over difficulties that begin with some physical disease and create psychological disorders. Chronic diseases such as diabetes or multiple sclerosis are clearly physical in origin and yet they produce psychological stresses in the lives of people diagnosed with these ailments. Acute diseases such as cancer may, and perhaps should, involve psychological as well as medical care.

Another argument against using the medical model to treat psychological disorders has little to do with the practice of medicine. It might be labeled objections to the myth of the medical model. If I take a medicine for a sore throat and my throat improves, I might reasonably say the medicine cured my sore throat. I would attribute the power to the medicine and not to myself. I might call it a "wonder drug." If the physician writes a prescription, it may never dawn on me that the physician has not ordered me to take the drug but has suggested that it might be of help. In the myth of the medical model, the patient is a passive recipient of treatment procedures about which he or she has no say and little understanding. The assumption is that the physician is in charge.

Consider a hospital scene. A patient is brought into the hospital emergency room. Routinely, an intravenous (IV) system is attached to the patient to provide a glucose and water solution to help maintain the person's strength and to make it easier to administer other drugs, if needed, through the IV. Of course, these procedures are not undertaken without someone's permission, but patients might never be aware that they have given permission in the various forms they have signed. They simply received the treatment.

15

In my own experience, I was scheduled for in-office surgery. The physician explained the procedures and ended by saying that after the operation I would be given a tranquilizer. I said I didn't think that would be necessary; he replied that it was part of the routine and in his experience, he had found it helpful. I expressed my thanks for his explanation and again said I probably wouldn't need it. He suggested that we wait until after the surgery to make the final decision and I agreed. After the operation, he asked if I was feeling any anxiety, queasiness, or nausea. I said no, and as we were walking down the hall, the physician said with some apparent amazement, "You really don't need a tranquilizer, do you?" I didn't. Such small medical procedures just don't bother me much. I don't have serious anxiety about them and remain calm throughout such procedures as blood tests, removal of stitches, or the surgical excision of a wart or cyst. I don't tend to worry much afterward, either. But I may be in the minority of patients who are able to resist the forceful, or even passive, suggestions of a physician. Most of us, perhaps through habit or assumption, simply do what we are told—passive subjects of the doctor's will.

Finally, according to the medical model, knowledge lies outside the patient. No knowledge, competence, skill, or even information is needed by the patient for the medical model to be used effectively. At least, that is the myth. Now, let me interject a cautionary note: I want to make it clear that I do not object to medicine. I do not advocate the denial of medical treatments or the avoidance of physicians and their care when we are physically hurt, and I am not among those who believe that any physical ailment, disease, or injury can be treated by the "power of the mind" or even by deeply held spiritual beliefs. I do believe in the success of antibiotics, surgery, and other medical practices. My argument here deals only and specifically with the metaphor we choose in exploring life difficulties—especially those that seem to be predominantly mental or emotional in origin—and the explanation we apply in understanding those difficulties. These myths, as I have labeled them, pose problems for a contrasting model.

Proponents of the psychological model would take exception to the medical treatment of emotional distress and to each of the myths discussed above. First, they would argue that anxiety, depression, traumatic reactions, grief, and other symptoms of distress are not diseases but mental disorders. The distinction is profound and important. If anxiety is not physically based, then treatment with drugs may numb psychological feelings while leaving untreated the situational and mental factors that caused the anxiety. Prescribing antidepressants for grief may numb pain, but it might also interfere with a person's capacity to work and live through the grief. Grief is not merely the passage of time, but of coming to terms with the loss.

Advocates of each of these models approach distress with a certain attitude, and this attitude dictates the metaphors they use. The medical model involves *curing,* which implies returning to health after a disease. The psychological model advocates *coping,* which implies continuous cognitive shifts and behavioral adjustments. Proponents of each seem to perceive the person in different terms. The medical model uses the designation *patient* to describe the person who seeks help. Those promoting the psychological model prefer *client* with its connotation of consumer or customer. Each has its shortcomings, but each also metaphorically represents the attitude of its theoretical model.

I have found six important areas of comparison between the medical and psychological models. First, the medical model seeks to cure the patient of disease. It seems to imply a model of equilibrium in which the patient is returned to a state of health that the disease disrupted. It conveys an end state that can be achieved and after which no further treatment is required. The psychological model suggests that the best outcome of psychotherapy is an attitude of coping. Coping implies a process of striving and adjustment. The client's problems may not be ended, but the client's ability to cope on more satisfactory terms with life have been enhanced. The client has new skills and understanding with which to manage the stresses of life.

Second, the medical model seems to view treatment as separate from life. Treatment is isolated and particular to the regimen prescribed by the physician. Treatment is viewed as a disruption of the daily routine; the most effective treatment is the one that can be discontinued most quickly. The psychological model defines coping as a part of life. Psychotherapists seek to understand the dysfunctional strategies used by a client and the reasons for their use; then they work with a client to construct new, more effective strategies. Treatment is integrated into the client's daily routine. It is considered most effective when it becomes an ongoing part of the client's life.

Third, the medical model is objective. Who the patients are, what their values are, what beliefs, attitudes, or convictions they hold are not the primary concerns of the physician. Young or old; male or female; black, white, or Asian descriptors might be considered important because these connect with certain symptoms; but whether a person is kind or cruel, rigid or open, pessimistic or optimistic have little reference in the medical model. The physician's task is to obtain a clear history and description of the physical symptoms of the patient. Based on the symptomology, a diagnosis is reached and a treatment prescribed. The psychological model leans more toward the subjective. The very characteristics deemed unnecessary in the medical model are central to understanding in the psychological model. A person's kindness or cruelty, rigidity or openness, and other qualities are the very stuff of psychotherapy and central to understanding the life of the person. It is the personal and the unique that lead to exploration and understanding. Treatment is not prescribed. It is mutually decided on, jointly created, and collectively planned.

In the fourth point of comparison, treatment in the medical model is authoritative. The patient relies on the knowledge and skill of the physician to diagnose and treat the illness. In this regard, the patient is passive. Patients may have little comprehension of the nature or genesis of their complaints, nor does such knowledge matter in treatment. Patients often do not understand the reasons or processes of the prescribed treatment. The psychological model is collaborative. The psychotherapist's knowledge is not about what should be done but in creating a climate in which the client may explore emotional issues, problems, and/or dilemmas in an atmosphere optimal to their resolution. In a nonthreatening climate, what was vague and undifferentiated can be seen with clarity and precision. Solutions and options present themselves when the issues, problems, and dilemmas can be examined undefended and undisguised. Often the psychotherapist need go no further. Given a clear understanding, most people are able to arrive at workable options for themselves. When this is not the case, the psychotherapist and client can construct coping strategies collaboratively.

Fifth, the view of the medical model is external. What counts is the physician's examination and the diagnosis that he or she draws. What patients think about the symptoms carries little consequence as patients typically lack the scientific training to develop an informed opinion. An interesting observation of physicians who have become patients is that their attending physicians discount the doctor-patient's medical opinions of their own symptoms as they are now in a patient role and are not considered objective. Patients are viewed from the outside and a judgment is made about their condition. Remedies are proposed and the patient is ordered to do what is prescribed.

The psychological model, on the other hand, tends to be internal. The point of view of the client is of paramount importance because the client's view is an important part of understanding for the psychotherapist. The very content and process of describing symptoms aids in understanding them. In the psychological model, what clients lack in scientific or technical knowledge is more than compensated for in their subjective knowledge of themselves. There is no better expert on the self than the "owner." To the degree that the psychotherapist can create a climate in which clients are able to express what they know of their own natures, clarity and understanding become possible. Taking an internal point of view, the psychotherapist is able to understand the decisions, fears, obstacles, and perspectives that have led clients to psychotherapy. This willingness to enter the private, subjective world of the client permits empathic understanding. From the perspective of the client, collaboration becomes possible because he or she does not feel judged or manipulated. The psychotherapist's proposed options feel comfortable and right precisely because they come from an understanding based on the reality of the client.

19

In the sixth and last comparison, the psychological effects of the medical model on the patient can range from detachment to disenfranchisement. Patients might actually believe the doctor cured them. There is little in the medical model to suggest otherwise. There is no institution, outside of a prison, in which people have less power than in a medical institution. A hospital is unmatched in treating people as if they were helpless. Patients are passive recipients of procedures they neither control nor understand. Power lies with the institution and the individual physician. Patient involvement is limited to giving permission for the physician to make decisions or to perform some specific function—much like giving a power of attorney. Someone else is now charged with making the decisions. The psychological model is meant to be empowering. The psychotherapist encourages clients to seek out personally meaningful solutions for themselves. The involvement of the psychotherapist in problem solving is limited to providing strategies for practicing some new option, skill, or other collaborative solution. Clients struggle through to some satisfactory resolution. In the struggle and its successful resolution, clients are strengthened by new knowledge and competence, and by a willingness to use these in their own behalf. They recognize that the power to change the issue that brought them to psychotherapy lies within them. They have, through the process of psychotherapy, empowered themselves.

In the psychological model, clients have not been cured of disease but have learned new strategies to cope with the struggles of their lives. They learn that these skills for coping can help them for the rest of their lives. They have become psychotherapists to themselves.

4

∾

The Source of the Hurt

*P*sychotherapy isn't concerned with the individual alone. It is not my intention to suggest that all issues, problems, or dilemmas begin within the individual. To believe that psychological distress always begins within the person is to "blame the victim" when the source may well be some other person, event, or cultural ill. What can be the source of the conflicts that require an individual to cope? In addition to understanding the degree of the injury, therapist and client must try to understand the seed and soil that produced the pain.

Some distresses do reside within the individual mind. These *intrapersonal* issues, problems, or dilemmas may begin in biology or in the mental constructions of a meager and deficient worldview. An issue might be shyness. There is something of a debate among helping professionals regarding the origin of shyness, but most line up on the side of biology or temperament. Shyness, however, need not cripple the social involvement of a person. It can, of course, create interpersonal, educational, social, and vocational complications if not addressed, but it can be overcome. It is a condition that need not ravage our lives.

Many entertainers, educators, executives, psychotherapists, public speakers, or others in the public eye have reported being shy. They have approached the situation as a matter of mastering a natural reaction in order to perform a specific task. A teacher might be reticent and withdrawn at a cocktail party but be a firecracker in the classroom. An actress might be soft-spoken and restrained in her personal life and portray a vamp or a frenzied terrorist in a movie. For others, their shyness is merely a matter of private concern that is little recognized by their associates. They perform their tasks and tolerate the anxiety they feel.

Sometimes, however, the inwardly experienced anxiety can be of such severity that the issue moves from a concern to a psychological problem. This might be the situation in a panic attack or agoraphobia, where interactions with others are seriously hampered or crippled by an inner, undefined anxiety.

Other intrapersonal matters can be problems in the life of a person. Many in our society consider homosexuality a formidable social problem. Others believe that homosexuality is not a matter of choice but rather of biological destiny and that the problem lies in society and not with the person. As the matter stands now, homosexuality creates adversity in the lives of many men and women. In psychotherapy, the problems explored may center on coping with the societal exclusion that results from homosexuality rather than on homosexuality itself. Psychotherapy may deal with the person's reaction to the exclusion, real or imagined. It may involve anger at society. It may involve puzzling over why one member of a family is heterosexual and another homosexual. What play of environment and heredity created that result? More disturbing for some may be the unwanted discovery that they believe they are the wrong gender. A man may believe he is a woman trapped in a man's body. This is not a dilemma that can be solved by psychotherapy alone, and there may be no satisfactory solution.

At birth, in cases of ambiguous secondary sexual characteristics, physicians are sometimes forced with making a determination of sex and surgically altering the baby to conform to that determination. Sometimes they make a wrong determination. If the mistake is discovered early, after a year or two, corrective surgery can be done with little psychological disruption. After that the evidence shows that psychological adjustment is problematic. Is this situation intensified when after years of life as a male, a person discovers that he is uncomfortable in a male body? It is well within the imagination to suppose that would be the case. Sometimes, though, even after surgery, a person may continue to struggle with psychological dilemmas in life. Our understanding is enhanced to know that some psychological matters begin in the self. Anxiety, depression, and even sexual choices may stem from biological or mental sources that have been little influenced by others. Even though this is the case, they often have satisfactory resolutions that involve relationships with others and the larger society.

Some life concerns have their origins in *interpersonal* influences. As young people mature, they are typically forced to face the rigors of dating or other forms of romantic engagement with their peers. These interpersonal issues can be painful, threatening, educational, and formative in our lives. Some navigate these interpersonal waters with native knowledge and feel the better for it. Others are left with lifelong personal insecurities. It is in the interaction and the meanings attributed to those interactions that our psychological structures can be influenced.

Many psychological theorists have, naturally, indicated that the most important interpersonal relationship of all is the parental one. Our parents' significance seemingly cannot be overestimated. Often, our early experiences with our parents propel us in one direction or another. Equally significant is the position of other psychological theorists who hold that our early experience with our parents, though critical, is not immutable, and that other, later, experiences may influence us for good or ill as well.

The source for much that is good and bad in our lives comes from our interpersonal associations. Someone once said that "doing your own thing" or always having your way was a great philosophy in a society of one! In real life, things have to be worked out with others. In the interplay between people, strife occurs. I once read a *Dear Abby* column in which a woman was distraught because her husband wore shorts on their vacation to Europe. I don't know where this couple's conflicting views of convention come from, but they are clearly in conflict. I don't know whether wearing shorts is a big deal or not (Abby said it was because some institutions in Europe have a dress code), but it was for this woman and her husband. We do not all view things from similar perspectives, and this is a source of friction for us. Such interpersonal matters can be causes of squabbles, arguments, fights, or wars.

In our society, the demise of the nuclear family unit is an ominous reality. The effect on society in general and on the members of the family in particular can be negative and chronic. Years after the divorce of their parents, a significant number of people point to this event as a source of disappointment, anger, and sorrow—even after they are adults. The scourge of physical and sexual abuse can destroy the future of its victims. Faith, trust, security, and the very possibility of subsequent loving relationships are threatened by this violation of a person. That it comes at the hands of parents and others who are the expected protectors of children shocks our sensibilities and troubles our souls. That people do survive abuse is a testament to the human will. Unfortunately, many do not. Some interpersonal acts do not have pleasant resolutions. Torture, murder, or senseless violence may so harm the surviving victims or surviving friends and family that their lives cannot find a peaceful path.

Beyond the influences of individuals, of friends, and of family there exists the intangible but compelling indoctrination of groups, society, and culture. These *impersonal* forces can be sources of psychopathology in the lives of people. If a Hispanic person comes to psychotherapy filled with rage over racism, a therapist may make a serious psychotherapeutic mistake in focusing on intrapsychic conflicts or early childhood influences. The most direct path may be to talk about institutional racism and the suppression of potential presented by discrimination. If a woman comes to psychotherapy and expresses a fear of success, the more appropriate course may be to examine cultural oppression rather than exploring her individual self-esteem. If a spouse is battered, of what use is suggesting that some aspect of her personality may be inciting the batterer? More likely, the acceptability of violence in the society or culture lies at the heart of this dilemma. The cruelest form of misunderstanding and misreading is to imply that sociocultural failings are somehow the flaw of intrapersonal structure or interpersonal interactions. Failing to address the perils of racism and sexism as more than matters of individual concern continues the pathological forces in the society. Viewing alcoholism as a personal flaw of an individual permits the forces that invite drinking to continue unmanaged. This is tantamount to treating gangrene with beauty cream; there may be some improvement in appearance, but the disease persists unchecked.

Impersonal matters, like intrapersonal and interpersonal ones, have degrees of concern. Negotiating with a bureaucracy may be an impersonal issue. Racism, sexism, and violence are problems that are difficult but not impossible to resolve. Poverty, alcoholism, and other forms of substance abuse defy solution. In these instances, people are more often victims than agents of cause. Psychotherapy that seeks to cope with impersonal matters—with concerns of groups, society, and culture—can be an exploration of empowerment for social change more than it is the investigation of inner and interactive forces.

Abraham Maslow, a seminal thinker and prominent psychologist, once proposed a category of mental disorders he called *metapathology*.[1] These *metapersonal* themes are universal, planetary, and abstract. They transcend the concern for an individual, a couple, or a family. They overshadow the regard for a single society and seek the good of all people all the time. These planetary issues might include a desire for an effective United Nations, a widely accessible world bank, or universal education. With metapersonal concerns, people would devote themselves to solving problems of the environment or population. They would sacrifice to triumph over world hunger, war, or human rights. They would transcend or suppress their own personal demons much as Abraham Lincoln is believed to have done to save the Union.

The self loses its importance in the face of universal needs. Spiritual leaders, perhaps before recorded time, have proclaimed the cosmic connection between all the sentient beings of the earth. Sacrificing themselves to their convictions, they have sometimes enlightened others and sometimes taken them to destruction in the practice of their fanaticism. Initially, the vision has been beyond the individual, beyond the family, beyond the society and the culture to the collective whole. There is both majesty and danger in such visions.

The task for the psychotherapist is to come to a point where the practical necessities of self-maintenance are balanced with honoring the person. It is likely that people with grandiose visions are

25

revealing their peculiar pathology, but the test of understanding is the ability to separate the real from the false. In the face of the real, *metapersonal* issues can be as painfully felt and be as deserving of understanding and a plan of action as any intrapersonal concern or interpersonal conflict.

The lives of people can be complex. Their struggles with the complications of existence can range from mild to severe. Some problems may have no solution. For some people, the source of the struggle may lie within themselves; for others, the cause springs from the culture or abstract, philosophical matters. Whatever its intensity and wherever its source, each struggle demands respectful attention.

5

On Change

*P*sychotherapy is a beginning, the beginning of change. Change is a process. This chapter is my attempt to describe the process of change as I have seen it in my clinical experience. I am not trying to be scientific in any strict sense here, although I am striving to be systematic. The ideas expressed are tentative, and I do not intend to imply that this is the only possible way one can conceptualize the process of change in psychotherapy. Many others have also examined change and have stated in both theoretical and research terms the nature of its process (Beitman, 1987; McConnaughy, Prochaska, & Velicer, 1983; McConnaughy, DiClemente, Prochaska, & Velicer, 1989; Steenbarger, 1992; Strong & Claiborn, 1982; Tracey & Ray, 1984).

People seem to go through different understandings of their lives as they come to grips with their own issues, problems, and dilemmas. Most appear to increase their ability to live effectively even in the face of continuing trials. Still, I believe most psychotherapists would describe the struggle people undertake in psychotherapy with words such as unfolding, evolving, progressing, developing, flowing, maturing, transforming, or adjusting. As I have witnessed this process, it has seemed to follow a similar path for the many who have taken it. This is a paradox for me because I know that no one way will serve everyone. Although each person has found his or her own way out of necessity, there appear to be commonalties as well. Let me show you the path that many have taken in their lives. Some have not walked the entire path; some have progressed with tortured deliberation; others have seen the way and confidently moved ahead. Psychotherapy is not a guarantee of change and there were some who did not venture far down the path.

Change begins in the recognition that something isn't working in one's life. Some part needs correction, adjustment, alteration, or outright ejection. To begin the process, one must *admit* that something is so. The word *admit* means to "permit to enter, to let in." It means to concede a fact, and that is all it means. It does not mean to approve of the fact or like it or agree with it. To admit means only that something is true or so. Entering psychotherapy doesn't necessarily mean that the person knows what is not working in his or her life. Exploration leads to that knowledge. It takes courage to admit that what has been discovered is true in his or her life. Admission is made to the self. Admission does not involve other people in any direct sense. By admission, a person tells himself or herself that the issue is actual and must be faced. Admission is the beginning of change.

To some extent, change must involve others, unless the issue involves true intrapsychic origins. It is just that so few issues involve exclusively intrapsychic origins. Given this, change requires disclosure of the facts of one's life to others. Disclosure doesn't mean that you have to "sell the family parrot to the town gossip." It means that the significant, relevant people who have a part in or will be impacted by the changes need to be informed. Those who have a need to know must be told. For change to occur, most of the time, the facts have to be *acknowledged* to others. Other people must be allowed to know that the client is struggling through a process of change. This is by no means as simple as it sounds. It is a significant step in the change process. One of the anomalies of emotional chaos is that people are often ashamed that they are experiencing it. People may not acknowledge their inner, emotional grappling even to the ones they love. Often, they behave this way from a desire to protect others by not acknowledging the inner storm, especially among people who believe their turmoil represents punishment for some real or imagined sin or failing—a not uncommon phenomenon.

Acknowledgment means recognizing that psychotherapy is not shameful and that change is possible. Acknowledgment is agreeing that one needs help, that others can and want to help, and that for them to do so, they have to know what is needed. To know this, they must be told. There is a difference between admitting to oneself that change is needed and acknowledging it to others. Acknowledgment allows others to respond accurately, acting on a statement of fact rather than on conjecture. It permits deeper clarity and identifies those in the environment who can be relied upon for support.

Change requires change. This seemingly redundant statement lies at the core of many failed processes. Exploring and understanding are not sufficient. It is necessary to act. Change requires *accommodation*. The word *accommodate* implies that one thing must be subordinated to another. Things have to be ordered. If a person recognizes his or her fear of public places, accommodation may mean two or three trips to the supermarket instead of one long trip. Accommodation may mean that people begin to train themselves in a series of steps just to cope with a problem, or that they go to the mall just to force themselves to go. Ultimately, accommodation may mean a more ordered life. It is inconvenient, but a necessary step in the process. It demands courage, perseverance, and creativity. Accommodation means the gradual process of giving up old ways and taking on new ones. Habit, fear, and psychological defenses are fierce opponents and do not willingly give up their entrenched styles of coping. Change comes grudgingly to most people, it seems, but each accommodation enables the next. As painstaking as the process seems, it becomes easier with each successful intervention, requiring less and less sacrifice. In the process of change, those who are changing reach the mountain top.

Now the process is different. It is no longer one of internal, personal change, but one of changing the environment to fit the individual's personal needs. The word *adapt* implies modifying the circumstance and/or context. With adaptation, the person begins actively to effect changes in the environment and negotiate assertively the changes needed. Consider the following example of a person diagnosed with multiple sclerosis.

Confined to a wheelchair, this person struggled with the limitations imposed by the disease. He was unable to pursue his love of gardening because planting and tending the garden were not possible from his wheelchair. In the midst of dealing with his losses and the accompanying depression and increasing isolation, he sought out psychotherapy. He worked his way through the process of admitting that the diagnosis was accurate and that his reactions to it weren't helpful; he acknowledged his diagnosis and personal struggles to his friends; he accommodated to needed supports for walking and to a wheelchair. He had done all that could be expected of him. He was still depressed and still missed gardening. What could be done?

The problem was that he could not get out of his chair to work the soil. His solution was inspired. If he couldn't get to the ground, then the ground would have to come to him. He hired a contractor to construct a walled-in garden with concrete pathways that made gardening accessible to him. Now he plants, waters, rakes, weeds, harvests, and does whatever else is necessary at wheelchair level.

I recognize this as an adaptation that involves technology, and adapting may mean using technology as one way for the person to get on with his life. Adaptation may involve technology, or scheduling, or timing, or lifestyle changes that are purposefully designed to help people live a life in which they can find pride, joy, and meaning. Adaptation means that people become active agents in their own lives and refuse to be victims of debilitating situations or past events. It means, at this point, that whatever brought them to psychotherapy is no longer a defining factor in their lives.

Development does not stop when psychotherapy ends. People continue the processes begun in psychotherapy. They *advance*. The word advance means to move forward. Years ago, interestingly enough, it meant *to lift up*. Beyond adaptation, beyond purposefully taking command of their lives, people discover a new purpose for life itself, a "cause" that may enrich them beyond their previous visions. Literally, they may have become more than they might have been without their successful struggle through the processes of admission, acknowledgment, accommodation, adaptation, and advancement. The struggle and resolution strengthened them, possibly bringing them to a more profound understanding of life. In this sense, their struggles in psychotherapy have served as catalysts, as flash points of change for their personal development. Tragedy may lead to strength. It can be a case of *ad astra per aspera* (to the stars through difficulties). In psychological theory, such development is labeled *actualization.*

None of this is meant to imply that psychotherapy is necessary or to suggest that tragedy in life is a blessing. A reporter once asked James Michener, the author, whether the difficulty he experienced as an orphan early in his life, having to live in rough and deprived conditions was actually a benefit to him as a writer. It is instructive to note that Michener's reply was that he would have had it the other way. To overcome adversity, to grow and develop in spite of mean circumstances, is admirable and inspirational. People who have discovered more profound meaning in life after having to cope with awful events can and do wish the events had never touched them. They have grown and discovered strengths never imagined. They have learned from their misfortunes. They do not, however, rejoice in them.

We need also to consider the opposites of the processes described above. The opposite of admission is denial, of acknowledgment is concealment, of accommodation is resistance, of adaptation is stagnation, of advancement is retreat, and of actualization is psychopathology. Make no mistake: The stakes are high in psychotherapy. Change calls for risks. Risks invite fear. Fear disrupts effort. To change, one must try. To try, one must have courage. Courage leads to change. Change leads to life involvement and possible fulfillment. Not to change leads to a life of denial, concealment, resistance, stagnation, retreat, and social disorganization. Each of us, whether involved in psychotherapy or not, must consider this progression.

6

On Listening

*P*icture this scene. A runaway youth has fallen in with a gang of thugs and terrorists who have captured a Great Teacher for cruel and nefarious purposes. He watches as they torture and seek to humiliate the Teacher. Touched by the Teacher's courage and inner strength, the youth shyly approaches the old Teacher. The Teacher says, "How can a face so young wear so many burdens?" The boy replies, "So, you can talk." The Great Teacher replies, "And I can also listen. Some say that the path from inner turmoil begins with a friendly ear. My ear is open if you care to use it."

Profound words. We should not be deterred from recognizing them merely because they come from a movie about sewer-dwelling mutated reptilian comic book characters and are spoken by a giant rat![1] Regardless of the source, these words do carry wisdom with them. An open ear can begin the process of healing for a troubled person.

A psychotherapist does not listen passively. Listening is active, energetic, dynamic, and purposive. As a person tells his or her life story, a psychotherapist listens for the ordinary, everyday, and expected content of any story—who, what, when, where, why, and how. Even this surface form of listening requires attention and purpose. The simple intensity of listening often surprises people. To be heard, even at the level of datum and fact, is sometimes an unexpected and pleasant relief for people. What is called sensitivity, insight, and intuition is often the appreciation and acknowledgment by the listener of what is genuinely substantial and compelling in the story.

In the flow of the story, how does one decide what is important and what is not? In listening for content, the psychotherapist listens for who, what, when, where, why, and how. In listening for the meanings, feelings, emotions, and significance, the psychotherapist is guided by two principles: *intensity* and *frequency*.

A person comes to a psychotherapist and says, "I just don't know what to talk about really. I know I am <u>ill at ease</u> in my <u>relationships</u> with people. I guess we could talk about my <u>parents</u>, or my husband, or my <u>father</u>, I guess, or my children, or my <u>mother</u>. I just don't know where to begin." The psychotherapist says, "So your relationship with your parents is tense and edgy. Anxious, perhaps?" Why did the psychotherapist decide to talk about parents? Where did this therapeutic reply come from? At one level, it involves the guidelines of listening to facts and data—the who, what, when, where, why, and how. Look at the underlined words above and then follow this short analysis.

WHO is identified as the client and the parents because of frequency.

WHAT is identified by the client as relationships.

WHEN is specifically unknown at this point, but is referred to in the present.

WHERE is unknown at this point.

WHY is labeled *tense, edgy,* and *anxious* to help clarify the meaning of "ill at ease."

HOW isn't presently known.

Why did the psychotherapist focus on the parents rather than the husband and the children? Possibly this particular psychotherapist theoretically focuses on parent-child relationships. Another therapist might have emphasized the role of the self in the client's discontent. In response to the client's words, this is an example of frequency. The "open ear" heard parents mentioned more frequently than others in the list. In a few short sentences, the psychotherapist knows a vague outline of who, what, why, and their relative importance. Additionally, the psychotherapist knows what other content information is needed—when, where, and how.

These principles of purposive listening lead the psychotherapist and the client to greater clarity and understanding. By themselves, the principles can be good servants of exploration and understanding. Practiced, they can lead to a foundation of cognitive and emotional knowledge of the origins, dynamics, and ineffectiveness of behavior that brought the person to psychotherapy. Nevertheless, there is more to listening than these techniques.

The language of facts and data is bland. It is unseasoned. In comparison, the language of meaning, emotion, and significance is peppered with allusions to consequences in the life of the person. An attentive psychotherapist listens to a person's word selections in telling the story. The language of turmoil is dramatic, emotional, metaphoric, and symbolic.

The ear of a psychotherapist is not only open; it is also trained. It has been taught to hear the ordinary informational flow of a story and to discern what is of substance in the story. To the educated ear of a psychotherapist, the language of turmoil reveals connections that might be unknown to the person seeking therapy. I realize that with this statement, many part company with the practice of psychotherapy. Some people simply do not believe they may be unaware of what is obvious to others. Yet, one of the assumptions of psychotherapy is that people might not be fully cognizant of their own internal motivations. To some extent, this is a matter of faith. On the other hand, it is demonstrable. One example widely given of incongruent behavior is of people who slam their fists down on the table and, with veins standing out on their necks and faces flushed, say, "I am *not* angry!" Well, you don't have to be a psychotherapist to know that if the person is telling the truth, then the fist is disconnected from the brain. A person talks and slams his or her fist down on the arm of the chair. This is *dramatic language*. It can thrust the person toward a deeper understanding of his or her own motivation when the psychotherapist acknowledges the act and calls attention to the discrepancy. The psychotherapist might say, "One part of you says that you aren't angry, and yet your fist says you are." This is not judgmental, evaluative, interpretive, or

35

even confrontive. It is descriptive. It is clear and it is genuine. Acknowledging the dramatic incongruity of the person's action and words offers the possibility of taking the psychotherapy into deeper, more profound intimacy with the person.

The language of turmoil is *emotional language*. There is a world of difference between saying, "I am ill at ease in my relationships" and saying, "My relationships suck!" An attentive psychotherapist would respond to the emotionality of that phrase "My relationships suck!" The psychotherapist might respond, "It isn't just that your relationships aren't going well. You sense them as disastrous and out of your control." Such a reaction on the part of the psychotherapist acknowledges the gravity of the statement and invites the person to recognize its power for the self as well. It encourages exploration.

The language used by the psychotherapist can "match" the style of language clients use to describe their lives. This behavior isn't crucial, but it is influential enough to mention. A psychotherapist also listens to the language *style* of the person. Language styles are typically given in *visual* (I see where you are coming from), *auditory* (I hear that), or *kinesthetic/physical* (I got you, or I can handle that) forms. It would not be matching to say, "I hear what you are saying" when the person has said, "Do you get the picture?" If a person says, "It is all buzzing, booming confusion," a psychotherapist typically would not say, "The picture is hazy for you." But, if the person says, "It is just buzzing, booming confusion," and the psychotherapist says, "It is deafening," this reply would be a match, even though it only paraphrases what the person has said and doesn't seem to provide any understanding of its meaning for the person.

In discussing a sense of rejection, people might say, "I feel rejected," or they might say, "I feel like I have been hit in the face with a wrecking ball." How much more exquisitely descriptive the second phrase is. It communicates the pain, damage, and force of the person's experience. In therapy, a person's use of *metaphoric language* is a clue that the level of importance has escalated. It is a cue to the therapist to listen harder, a tip that something important is being said. The phrase, "I feel rejected," signals that more exploration is needed because there is no clear indication of the meaning the person attaches to this phrase. With the second statement above, however, the significance is clear, and the person has provided the psychotherapist with suggestions for moving the psychotherapy forward.

In two of the examples above, there were symbolic references. In the example of drama, the person said, "My relationships suck!" In the example of metaphor, the person said, "I feel like I was hit in the face with a wrecking ball." *Symbolic language* is an opening into the unrecognized meanings of behavior. Let me urge a caution, however, in examining symbolic language. It is important that your interpretations remain tentative. Such language may or may not be communicating hidden emotional meanings. It is important, nevertheless, to stay open to the idea that exploring language with the person may stretch the therapy to greater understanding.

Let's look at the first example: "My relationships suck!" What can be the symbolic meaning of the word *suck*? It might be merely a slang term connoting *bad*. A psychotherapist might consider ideas like "sucking air," which might mean that the person is exhausted by his or her relationships (as when a runner is overextended and is trying to catch his or her breath). It might be extended to mean "suckle," in which the person feels dependent on others in his or her relationships (the way a baby is dependent on a breast-feeding mother). The person may be denied succor and find no nourishment in relationships.

In the second example, the person said, "…hit in the face…," not "hit in the chest," "hit in the stomach," or "hit in the head." The client said "face." People do not use the words they use by accident. This is another reason psychotherapists listen attentively to what people say. Their words do communicate. In this case, what can be the symbolic importance of the word *face* over other possible words? I might think this way. What is the most recognizable part of a person? I would conclude that it is the face. If a person is hit in the face, the most recognizable part of the person has been damaged. It may be that identity itself has been assaulted. Another understanding might be that the person has been defaced, insulted, or diminished by relationships. In examination of the symbols a person uses, meanings that are are motivating behavior may be uncovered.

A psychotherapist's training, willingness, and skillful listening allow him or her to be of service to a person. All these elements permit nonthreatening exploration, deeper understanding, and, ultimately, a clearer path for both the psychotherapist and the person seeking help.

7

On Courage

There is much unhappiness in the world. Even the most well adjusted of us still face tragedy. Life leads inevitably to death. The most blessed of us who grow up with loving parents, in sound relationships, in fulfilling careers, and with wholesome friendships face the death of the ones we love as parents age or accidents strike. We may face the destructive forces of violence, disease, or drugs as people we love are senselessly destroyed by forces that defy understanding and comprehension.

Psychotherapy demands courage—from both the person seeking help and the psychotherapist. Courage is the mental and emotional willingness to persevere in the face of fear. Psychotherapy is often a fearful process. I am sometimes asked if I don't get tired of the people who come for therapy. Carl Rogers, one of the best-known psychotherapists in the United States, perhaps in the world, proposed *unconditional positive regard* (a nonjudgmental, respectful attitude toward the persons who come for psychotherapy) as one of three prerequisites for effective psychotherapy.[1] How, some ask, can one feel positive about people who come in week after week to whine and complain about their lives? In fact, I don't see people who whine and complain. I see people coming in to do something about their lives. A physical analogy might serve the point here. A client in psychotherapy is somewhat like a person who has broken his or her leg and has come to have it set. The problem is that there is no anesthetic. The person has to bear the pain as the leg is set. Then, the next week the leg has to be broken and set again. The person does that week after week. There is no anesthetic for emotional pain, no pain killer for grief. I don't resent people who come for psychotherapy. I don't grow tired of them. They are not whiners or complainers. They are people of courage. I admire them. I admire their courage. Many of them do return week after week knowing that they are going to feel emotional pain as they grapple with their personal anguish.

Others might say that some people bring trivial or inconsequential issues to psychotherapy. These people, they say, just need to "get a grip" or "suck it up" and recognize that the world isn't any bed of roses. Others might say that people just have to *accept* things and get on with their lives. This sort of advice seems to come most often after diagnosis of chronic disease, divorce, or other life disasters. It comes, that is, in the face of the difficult, messy, and miserable times of life that can frighten others and cause them to withdraw just when we need them the most. They may defend themselves by claiming that we are overreacting to a life predicament.

Of course, some people do come into psychotherapy for what many would label "trivial" events. One of our fundamental misunderstandings of human emotions is that we place psychological importance on the event and not the person's reaction to it. For some, the difficulty is not in recognizing the reality of the event so much as it is in coping with the personally felt pain of the event. Sometimes advice advocating "acceptance" can be cruel; it sends a message that the person's emotional response is what others want them to change. When "accept" means "don't feel the way you do," its message is emotionally unhelpful.

The word *accept* may be one of the most used and most misunderstood words in the helping professions, such as psychotherapy, medicine, and the ministry. It is, in these professions, a technical word, a jargon word. Perhaps we have used it for so long and so sloppily that even we, in the helping professions, have forgotten that it has an ordinary, nontechnical meaning. I invite you to look up the word in a dictionary. You will find that the word *accept* means to receive or approve willingly. Now, it seems an act of supreme callousness to ask or tell people confronted with a life misfortune that what they have to do is willingly receive and even approve of the news that their lives are tragically altered. In its technical us-age, the word *accept* means only that something is a fact, that it is so. It does not mean to approve, to agree with, or to be resigned to, willingly or otherwise. Herein lies the difficulty. Technical language is useful in communicating with others in the same field. Outside that field, jargon often can miscommunicate. It may only confuse listeners, as they may or may not understand the nature of the terminology. (One need only to visit a local computer store to ex-perience this frustrating phenomenon.) The general public may have heard a psychotherapist use the word *acceptance* in some public forum, such as one of the many talk shows on television, or on a radio program featuring a psychologist; but they often do not real-ize that it has a specialized meaning. The audience hears the every-day meaning of the word whereas the psychotherapist means the technical usage. Even with good intentions in giving such advice to others, we can hurt them by telling them to "accept" their misfor-tune.

One more point: Whatever public misunderstanding may exist around this word, psychotherapists are not in the business of giv-ing advice to people in any case. Even though it does happen, psy-chotherapists have completely forgotten the purpose of psycho-therapy when they advise people to accept (in its more common usage) their plight.

Returning to the topic of courage, some might say we live in the "age of victims" in which all of us have been abused in some way and believe we need therapy. Consider an analogy: To a trout not hooked, the behavior of a trout caught on the hook and line of an angler must seem strange indeed. The thrashing, jumping gyra-tions of a hooked trout must seem irrational and out of control to one not hooked because the line is invisible in the water. Yet, from the point of view of the hooked trout, its behavior is perfectly ratio-nal and, in fact, the only behavior that seems open to it, given its situation. This viewpoint may well represent people in psychologi-cal distress.

This analogy helps to clarify the obligation of psychotherapists not to judge others but to seek diligently to enter their world to understand the particular hook that is causing them to struggle

41

against their invisible angler. Just as one might see the turmoil of the thrashing trout as irrational, this same behavior seen from another perspective may be viewed as a courageous struggle to free itself from overly controlling adversities. The struggle demands courage, and frequently, in struggling, people discover within themselves the substance with which to fight and to face their life dilemmas.

Psychotherapists must also find the courage within themselves to accompany their clients into the sometimes frightening chronicles of their lives. More than just accompanying, a psychotherapist must have the courage to seize the therapeutic moment. Sometimes a therapist knows that to progress and unravel an experience will provoke pain. Such times are often moments of clarity for those seeking help. A psychotherapist who avoids them does not help, but becomes one more impediment to advancement for his or her clients. Understand that it is the exploration and not the pain itself that is essential.

Gains may be made without pain, but sometimes gains can be made only in spite of pain. Pain is not the teacher. The knowledge and understanding that come from exploring one's life are the elements that teach.

How should a psychotherapist proceed in the face of fear and pain? Lead with your heart and go gently. Use compassion in touching the tender and fearful parts of a person's life. Acknowledge the fear. Recognize the pain. Tread softly. Handle the life of another with respect. Appreciate courage. Allow time for learning, profit, and gain. I don't entirely believe in the cliché "no pain, no gain," but I do believe that pain without gain is senseless. Consider carefully whether the anticipated pain has the potential for gain. If it does, then that is when a psychotherapist must have courage.

Being a psychotherapist demands other aspects of courage. One is the willingness to examine your own life for those aspects that might hold threat or danger. Personal knowledge of your own tender places is necessary if you are going to be of service to others as they endeavor to cope with their fears. In the struggle to open your heart to another, it may be necessary to have already confronted the formidable clash between fear and courage in your own life.

Another face of courage is the willingness of psychotherapists to immerse themselves in the emotional experience of life itself— to be involved in life in a reflective, contemplative, integrative, and self-searching way. Some of us are "wounded healers" who have also experienced a shattering side of living. Some have been wounded, lived through the experience, and matured. Others, who have not lived through trying life experiences, may immerse themselves in the emotional experiences offered by plays, films, novels, poetry, biography, and history. Whether through personal or vicarious experience, touching life in emotional depth seems clearly to be an act of courage necessary for a vigorous and effective psychotherapist.

8

On Caring

*W*e can help strengthen people or we can make invalids of them. Fred Richards, a psychotherapist, has written eloquently concerning a paradox of psychotherapy:

> I speak here of two ways of caring in the world. One is *caring for*. The other, *caring about*. *Caring for* is a matter of providing for or looking after. If I care for you, you are the object of my concern. I express my concern for you by taking charge of your life. When I care for, I feel most needed when you are an invalid and in need of my care. I feel most needed when you are in need. If I *care for* you, I see you as an object. Reducing you to an object, I invalidate you as a person. When I experience you as an object, I feel more secure and comfortable. You do not touch my life. You seem more predictable. You are much easier to control. *Caring about* is a matter of going out of one's self to meet the other fully. If I *care about* you, I meet you as a person. You matter in my world. In a sense, I stand naked before you. I wear no mask. I hide behind no role. We meet. And in the moment of meeting, we are free to discover our humanity. When I care about, I see you as a person. I see you as a person in process, growing, becoming. You are never quite the same. You are always new. Experiencing the newness of you, I am also freed to unfold and be who I am. We see one another as persons. We are not displaced. We are not invisible. We are free to be present and real. Every

situation is an opportunity to *care for* and *care about*. Every dialogue, every meeting, every moment is an invitation, calling out to ourselves to go beyond *caring for*. If I *care about* you, the appearance of *caring for* is lifted into love. If I fail to *care about* you, my *caring for* diminishes both of us.[1]

I know that some will say these are only words—and they are right; these *are* only words. The attitude that underlies the words, however, is the difference between a psychotherapist who respects and empowers people and one who insults and diminishes them. A psychotherapist who *cares for* a person regards that person as helpless. Think for a moment of the language we use, and perhaps how we feel, regarding people who are unable to manage for themselves. We might use language like, "I just have to do everything for him," or "Poor thing, she is as helpless as a kitten," or "Well, of course, he tries but, poor dear, he just doesn't have a clue about how to take care of himself." Psychotherapists might not use such language, but they might communicate other, equally damaging ideas. They might categorize persons—for example, "Well, he is dysfunctional." They might declare some to be incompetent—"Of course, she is out of touch with reality." They may use labels—"In my opinion, he is a victim of a personality disorder." The very words themselves are insulting. More to the point, if such an attitude prevails, it will obstruct the prospect that the person will develop the ability to take care of himself or herself. Thus, an attitude of *caring for* can create emotional invalids. Their psychological strength invalidated, they are in an eternal convalescent home constantly in need of the care of others. You do not help build the physical strength of others by lifting the barbell for them. They have been denied the probability, if not the possibility, of developing into autonomous human beings. They are subjected to the indignity of being considered weak, incapable, and inept. They are maligned by those sworn to be of service to them. Therein lies the aberration.

Psychotherapists who *care about* the people who seek their help communicate a different message. Psychotherapists who *care about* others communicate a sense of respect. These therapists provide a recognition of person's strengths and invite them to use those strengths in coping with the adversities of their lives. An important addition is that *caring about* includes *caring for* when it is appropriate and necessary. It includes nurture, support, guidance, and sustenance when essential. Consider a group of hikers on a mountain. If one slips and breaks a leg, it is perfectly reasonable for the others to carry the injured hiker down the mountain for emergency care. It is reasonable that while the person is in a cast, a friend might run his errands. Anyone who cares would lend a helping hand. But there will come a time when they recognize that in spite of the inconvenience and pain, the person will have to start walking on his or her own. *Caring about* means permitting people to walk on their own. It means taking the extra time needed for people to get into and out of the car, to make their way into the restaurant or movie. In using their own developing abilities, people are strengthened. If people are supported when they require it, guided when they need it, and continually allowed to discover and use their own personal resources, they leave psychotherapy able to cope more successfully with the dilemmas of their lives. Providing this environment is an expression of genuine compassion by the psychotherapist. It is the optimal and expected course and outcome of psychotherapy.

9

On Being Tough and Tender

*P*sychotherapy is not for the weak. It demands strength and courage. It is not a passive, flaccid endeavor. A psychotherapist must be *tough*. Paradoxically, he or she must also be *tender*. *Tough* psychotherapy is concrete, challenging, and confrontive. *Tender* psychotherapy is empathic, compassionate, accepting, and non-judgmental.

Psychotherapy must be *tough* because problems, psychopathologies, and defenses are tough. Psychotherapy must be *tender* because people are bruised and vulnerable. Because defenses are tough, the emotions of the person may be underdeveloped (delicate). Thus, psychotherapy must be *tender*.

It is this *both/and* approach to psychotherapy that enables the psychotherapist both to acknowledge the pain experienced by another and to challenge the person to struggle for understanding of and solutions to that pain. Both concepts, *tough* and *tender*, have specific importance. They represent the two wings of psychotherapy. If the psychotherapy is to fly, then it must be both *tough* and *tender*.

A psychotherapist who is merely *tough* is an emotional bully who seeks to intimidate vulnerable people. Such psychotherapists may derive some personal satisfaction from their rough, hard, or stern approach, but any therapeutic gain that occurs in their clients is more likely attributable to accidental successes than to any consistent, predictable therapeutic outcome.

A merely *tender* psychotherapist is an agent of the client's problems and defenses. Such psychotherapists may derive some satisfaction from viewing themselves as kind and caring people, but they may also unwittingly collude with the defenses of the person in maintaining or continuing the problem. Failing to challenge, the psychotherapist may encourage the client to avoid factual issues or may reinforce the client's feelings of inadequacy and frailty. For these reasons, psychotherapy must be both *tough* and *tender*.

People come to psychotherapy in a state of vulnerability. By entering psychotherapy, they have testified that the problems and defenses in their lives have been tougher than their present ability to cope. The psychotherapist must be *tough* so as to challenge their fears, defenses, cognitive mistakes, and/or discrepancies that appear in the course of psychotherapy. There are a number of reasons that a psychotherapist must be *tough*.

First, toughness is needed. Problems, issues, dilemmas, and/or psychopathologies are resistant. The psychotherapist must be tough if he or she is to help clients learn to cope effectively with life's problems and with psychological defenses. As a psychotherapist, you must make clear to your client that it is the problems and defenses that we are tough with and *not* with the client. The essential person is not being challenged; instead, a block to that person's effective living is being cracked and pushed aside, if possible, to make way for a better life. This is an important distinction; keep it foremost in mind when you are being tough in any therapeutic encounter.

Second, toughness is expected. By coming to therapy, clients are testifying that their problems are tougher than they are. Clients also believe that psychotherapists are even more tenacious than their problems. Therefore, psychotherapists who fail to demonstrate requisite courage and emotional experience disappoint their clients who are desperately seeking someone tougher than their problems.

Third, toughness is needed to achieve clarity. If the word and concept *defense* means anything in psychological terms, it means a barrier to a clear view of causality. Defenses distort reality. Defenses also preclude the opportunity for choice by limiting experience. One may argue the nature of reality and the importance of external or internal reality, but most psychotherapists agree that defenses, as mechanisms or as constructs, interfere with a client's clear understanding of his or her particular behaviors. Dealing with defenses offers the hope of clarity.

Fourth, toughness models effectiveness in dealing with problems and defenses. A psychotherapist who looks with the client at problems and defenses models an effective strategy for living. The psychotherapist who is tough enough to look at problems and defenses with a client demonstrates that such action is possible. That experience itself can be a powerful force for change.

Fifth, toughness implies that change is possible. Change becomes possible when problems and defenses are challenged or confronted in a tough therapeutic encounter. Clients come to therapy in a state of incongruence, testifying that their problems have overwhelmed their strategies for living. A congruent psychotherapist creates the conditions for change through therapeutic toughness.

By mastering these five aspects of tough therapy, a psychotherapist can become a more effective advocate for a client. The psychotherapist can be viewed as strong enough and brave enough to help the client confront defenses and deal with problems, dilemmas, and/or psychopathologies. Thus, through "appropriate toughness," the therapist can participate in the design and implementation of solutions.

And yet, tenderness is needed. People who enter psychotherapy are vulnerable. The therapist must help them confront and deal with problems and defenses, but he or she must also recognize that vulnerable people are easily injured. An analogy might be when we recognize that a hammer isn't the best tool to use to remove a splinter. If the psychotherapist is to be accepted as an advocate for the self-worth of the client, he or she must handle the tender, sore places of the client's life with gentleness and care. By such demonstrations of gentleness and care, trust is built. Psychotherapists demonstrate respect for clients by their ability to gently and tenderly examine their clients' injuries. It is important to recognize that precision and gentleness are not mutually exclusive. Let's now examine five specific reasons for *tender* psychotherapy.

First, in being tender, the psychotherapist recognizes that the client is wounded. Whatever our good intentions, when we handle a wounded person roughly, we run the risk of doing additional damage. If a person has a broken leg, forcing that person to walk will worsen the fracture. To treat the injured person tenderly can help prepare him or her for the pain of having the leg set, with the knowledge that healing will follow. So it is in psychotherapy. Rapport, trust, or confidence are gained by early gentleness.

Second, initial tenderness facilitates later toughness. This initial gentleness is not a manipulation of the client. It is evidence of *caring about* the client. It shows genuine concern as well as the expert recognition that later sessions may have to deal more toughly with injured parts of the person.

Third, the client is inexperienced. The person may be inexperienced in the effective use of emotions and of cognitions. His or her defenses have prevented full use of the emotions and clear thinking in the past. As with any inexperienced person, he or she must travel the way to success slowly and with care.

Fourth, the client may be naive. Clients may be people who believe they do not have the strength to deal with life's problems. They may have lost touch with or may have never developed the capacity for coping. Additionally, they may be blind to their own defenses that are preventing effective change in dealing with problems.

Fifth, you must be tender because a guiding moral principle of our profession is "Above all, do no harm." However our task is conceived, in no way is it proper for us to send clients back into the world more damaged than when they came to us for help. *Appropriate tenderness* presents the least potential for personal harm. There is no guarantee, of course, that the process of psychotherapy will help, but care can be given to ensure that the relationship itself and the methods employed in the psychotherapy are optimally created and employed to lessen the potential for harm.

Through mastery of these five aspects of tender therapy, a psychotherapist may become a competent healer, gentle enough to approach the wound, precise enough to accurately identify the harmful agents, and skilled enough to treat without creating additional harm.

How do you know whether you are appropriately tough? What is appropriate toughness? The answer to these questions does not lie so much in behavior as it does in the intentions and purposes of the psychotherapist. When using psychotherapeutic toughness, we must emphasize the therapeutic nature of the intervention, not the toughness itself. A psychotherapist who uses toughness as its own end is an emotional bully. What confounds this issue for many is the observation that effective therapy is often tough. Effective therapy is difficult for both the client and the therapist. It is painful for the client and demands courage from the therapist. In the observation of effective therapy and in the discussions of effective therapists, only the toughness may be apparent. What emerges from effective therapeutic toughness, however, is clarity and ownership. What emerges from mere toughness is client dependence and defensiveness.

When the therapist is merely being tough, therapy is aggressive. He or she will use moralizing and manipulation. Disapproval and power become issues. Often inappropriate toughness may take subtle forms. The therapist might look sideways at a client to indicate disbelief. Any number of looks or stares may be intimidating.

Inappropriate toughness also occurs when, for some reason, the therapist becomes personally involved in being right, pursuing a personal value issue, or insisting that an interpretation be accepted by the client. Inappropriate toughness occurs when the psychotherapist has unwittingly become more interested in being tough than in being therapeutic.

Appropriate tenderness seems to occur when the therapist shows a respectful willingness to listen to the client. More important than passive listening is the struggle to understand clients in all their pain, confusion, and richness. Understanding carries a requirement that the therapist believe in the potential of clients to change.

Appropriate tenderness demands that a psychotherapist listen to each client's story with a practiced but not jaundiced ear. Appropriate tenderness recognizes and accepts the pain and confusion of clients and carries with it a respect for the strength and ability of clients to face and find solutions to the problems and defenses of their lives.

When is therapy "inappropriately tender"? The answer involves determining whose needs are being met. If the focus is on the therapist's need to be seen as a tender and caring therapist, then there is danger. The likelihood is that no substantive therapy is going on; the therapist is trying not to "go too fast" or "not to provoke unnecessary pain." However this reluctance is phrased, the client suffers because no genuine therapy is occurring. The therapist, the problems, and the defenses are all conspiring against the client to ensure that nothing sensitive is discussed. The effect of inappropriately tender therapy may be comforting for the therapist and the client, but the outcome is likely to be dependency, validation of the client's defenses, and the continuation of ineffective life skills. Tenderness is inappropriate when the need of the therapist to be seen as gentle and caring prevents the challenge of the client's problems and defenses. Emphasizing toughness over tenderness or tenderness over toughness results in different problems but similarly ineffective psychotherapy. Psychotherapists who are appropriately both *tender* and *tough* are working hard to create the conditions under which material, lasting, and positive psychotherapeutic change may take place.

54

10

On Being Close;
On Being Separate

*P*sychotherapy is not an antiseptic alliance. It is intimate. It is an intimacy of intellect and emotion, and in its intimacy, there is balance. It is a liaison unique in human relationships, in which one person is more known than the other. It is a meeting of two people in which the need of one is the focus. One is vulnerable and, in some degree, out of touch with his or her inner resources. Many psychologists label this a state of incongruence. It is a collaboration in which the psychological benefits are to be accrued by only one member of the affiliation. Yet, as intimate as this encounter is, one of the participants is in a state of vulnerability and reveals the details and pain of his or her life to the other. The purpose of the relationship is not intimacy itself—not companionship, friendship, or familiarity. Concern flows primarily in one direction. The investment in, the trust in, and the reliance on one of the partners by the other may be deep. As caring, as intimate, as intensely personal as this relationship is, it is temporary. The purpose of this peculiar association is the development of a sense of personal power in the person seeking help.

This distinctive characteristic of a therapeutic relationship is labeled *detached concern.* To help others, psychotherapists must be close to their clients, must understand. To understand, psychotherapists must reach out with compassion, with all their undisguised care, with experience, regard, and passionate commitment. This is the *closeness* concern. In the midst of this intimate encounter, however, each psychotherapist must also be keenly aware that the pain being visited and the chaos being touched resides in the other person. Psychotherapists must constantly remind themselves that it is the other person who is distressed or disoriented. This is the *separateness*/detachment.

In the study and practice of psychotherapy, the proper blending of these ingredients is one of the most difficult lessons. Its mastery is what permits the consistent and reliable practice of a psychotherapist. Those who err on the side of closeness burn up with the emotions they have taken in as they listen to people day after day. Those who err on the side of detachment become calloused to the pain of the people who seek their help. The balance is delicate and involves compassion and reflection.

Psychotherapists who move too close might sympathize and begin to feel their clients' pain. The resulting depression can affect their lives. Some might identify with clients and seek to comfort them or take charge of their struggles. A psychotherapist who moves too close might confuse concern with affection or psychological intimacy with physical intimacy. Romantic love and sexual encounters can easily be dangerous misuses of the intimacy of psychotherapy.

Psychotherapists may go to the other end of the continuum and become aloof. They may travel a path that begins in compassion, moves to carelessness, evolves into callousness, and ends with cruelty. In the need to protect themselves, some psychotherapists may withdraw behind a role of expertise, merely presenting the appearance of care without any of its substance.

Some therapists have retained so little investment in the psychotherapeutic partnership that they merely go through the motions. Because they have so little interest in the lives of people, they have no need to withdraw; they are not involved in the first place. They have become indifferent spectators rather than involved participants. They may be recorders of the human experience, but what they report seems to have no importance for them. They merely put in their time, and human experience seems to offer only boredom.

The harmonious resolution of this dilemma of closeness and separateness lies in the balance of caring, closeness, and protective distance. Successful therapists will have an appreciation of the difference between sympathy/identification and empathy. They will know with confidence that in psychotherapy, empathy helps and sympathy does not. They will be aware that the power of change lies within the client and not with the psychotherapist. They will recognize that the affection of clients in psychotherapy can be seductive, and link this knowledge with the humility of knowing that people seeking help are not much different from those offering it. Mastery of the closeness and distance paradox reminds us over and over again that just as the life of the person seeking help belongs to that person, the life of the psychotherapist belongs to the psychotherapist. It does not belong to the client's problems or psychopathology. In a science fiction television series,[1] the guiding principle of the space explorers was noninterference with any other culture or species they might discover. It was known as the Prime Directive. The crew was duty and honor bound to permit any discovered species to develop on its own. It was recognized that in coping with difficulties the strength of cultures and species grew. It is much like that in psychotherapy.

57

11

What the Mind Can Imagine

The best answer to an imaginary problem is a magical solution. Behind this seemingly nonsensical sentence lies the heart of psychotherapy. Many years ago, when our oldest son was about four years old, he came into our bedroom late at night and woke me. "Daddy, there is a monster in my room," he said. As you can imagine, this was most troubling news. Monsters have no business interrupting the sleep of children. Something had to be done.

For many, the years from two to six may be viewed as the romantic years of childhood. They can also be the most fearful times for children. These are the years in which children are mastering the separation between fantasy and reality. The lines are murky and unstable. A dream is as frightening as the corporeal fiend itself. Dreams, of course, frighten adults as well. The difference is that adults, when they awaken, know they have experienced only a dream. Identifying the difference does not provide much comfort for small children because the difference between a dream and the waking state (fantasy and reality) is not established for them yet. It is exactly the developmental task with which they are struggling.

And so, I had a four-year-old frightened by a monster late at night. What to do? "Well," I said, "we can't have this. Monsters aren't welcome in our house unless they are good monsters like the Cookie Monster. It will just have to leave."

"But it won't," our son persisted; "it hides in the closet and only comes out in the dark."

"Then we need something very special to get rid of it. I have just the thing. I have a bottle of Monster Spray in the kitchen. Monsters hate this stuff. It makes them sick. They won't stay around any place where it has been sprayed," I explained. And with that, I put a little bit of green food coloring and water into a small spray bottle and our son dutifully sprayed all the places in his room where a monster might hide. We slept peacefully that night and for the nights in the future, too. Every night before bed, our son would responsibly spray his room and no monsters came around. We talked about dreams and how they could entertain us. We talked about troubling dreams and what to do about them. I told him that our dreams belong to us and that if they scare us too much, it is within our power to change them. After a time, he no longer sprayed his room each night. It wasn't necessary. Whatever magic was in the bottle had transferred itself to him.

There is an epilogue to this story. Months later, our telephone rang and a friend said that some fantasy beast had occupied his daughter's bedroom and she wouldn't go to sleep. What was that stuff at our house that our son had told his daughter about? I explained the formula for Monster Spray and the reasoning behind it and guaranteed that the beast would be vanquished. Thirty minutes later the telephone rang again. Our friend said that the Monster Spray hadn't worked. His daughter said that only our son had real Monster Spray! He drove over to our house, picked up our well-used bottle, and true to expectation, his daughter sprayed her room and then calmly and peacefully went to sleep.

Aside from the fact that this story is cute and it is about our son, it can be instructive. It takes us into a psychological understanding of human beings' relationship with experience. This is a heavy burden for a spooky dream and a small child, yet that is the task we will undertake now. In the beginning of this chapter, I said the best answer for an imaginary problem is a magical solution—but what is real and what is imaginary? Most of us use the word *imaginary* to mean fictitious or nonexistent; we use *real* to mean material or tangible and even sensible. To say that another person's problem is imaginary is to dismiss it as unworthy of serious attention. For many, that is the difficulty they face in trying to explain their psychological pains to others. They are often told, "It is only in your head."

What is real? Here is the paradox. In psychotherapy, it is often the imaginary that is real. Go back to the story of the monster and our son. Did it frighten him? Did it interrupt his sleep? Did it drive him to seek help? Yes, of course. Was it real? Yes, it was real in the image. It is not real in the sense that some fleshy monster was in the room, but the fear was real and that is what psychotherapy deals with. This is the reality of thoughts and emotions. To say things are otherwise is an act of supreme arrogance. To deny the emotional reality of another is a failure of compassion and of the memory. We will not acknowledge their pain and we have forgotten our own fearful moments.

There is more to the potential of the imagination than helping a little boy through a frightening dream. There is nothing more powerful than the imagination. There is no obstacle that cannot be overcome in fantasy. In psychotherapy, what cannot be gained in reality can be gained in fantasy. A woman who had been raped when she was a nineteen-year-old was now in her thirties, still plagued by memories and nagging discontent with her life. The therapy moved through her retelling of her fear, shame, and guilt. Each, in its turn, was explored for its place in her unsettled life—justifiable fear that lingered to interfere with new relationships, irrational shame that had much more to do with others than with her, and unnecessary guilt concerning her own vulnerability. Each, after a time, took its place as important but no longer central to her continuing restiveness. She knew that her fear had been real and justified. She understood that her feelings of shame came from her enculturation in a society where sexual issues are always a matter of gossip, myth, and moralizing. She had made her peace with that. She knew she had done nothing wrong. Guilt had worked its way through her psychological system just as an infection might work its way through her physical system. What was the lingering interference? It came to this. She was alone, asleep in her apartment, when her attacker broke in and raped her at knife point. Even though she screamed, no one came to help her. No one came to her aid. And I said, "What would you have liked to have happen?" She said,

61

through her tears, "I just wanted someone to save me. I just wanted someone to come and help me." I said, "Close your eyes. Imagine the scene just as it happened that night except that this time, in your imagination, you will get the help you want." This is her fantasy.

I am asleep in my apartment when I am awakened by a man. He is straddled across me and has a knife at my throat. He is telling me to keep quiet or he will kill me. Even as I start to scream, he muffles my scream with his hand. I feel frightened, helpless, trapped. Suddenly, the door bursts open and this big, Irish cop is standing in the doorway. "Now what in the name of the bless'd saints would be goin' on here. You wouldn' be thinkin' of harmin' that poor girl would ya, lad? Now you know we can't be havin' the likes of that bein' done by the likes of you, now can we?" The man jumps off me and runs to the window. The big cop grabs him and says, "Ah, you poor demented fool. You can't be runnin' away." As he grabs him by the neck, he holds him out the second floor window, "Now you'll have to be droppin' your knife and . . . oh, Saints preserve us! I've dropped the poor boy. Oh my and he's landed on me patrol car. Now that's damagin' public property. There is goin' to be hell to pay down at the station." And he turns and looks at me and says, "Now, sweet girl, you go on back to sleep and I'll go down and check me patrol car to make sure there's no serious damage and haul this brigand off to the cell."

All was done in an Irish brogue, with dramatic voice and gestures—and here she began to laugh and cry. For a brief moment in psychotherapy, the world was as it should be. The innocent were protected; the guilty were punished. Poetic justice had been done and in this therapeutic moment, she could believe that the world consisted not only of the cruel but of protectors as well. Reality did not have to mean she was alone in the world. It did not have to mean the world was pitiless and indifferent. As frightening as her experience was, it could have been different. The way it had been did not mean that it always had to be that way. She could believe

62
∽

that she was worthy of protection. She could know that it was circumstance alone that had prevented her rescue. It was not that her world and the people who populated it would not help if they could. And that realization made all the difference. There was some work left, of course, to talk and sift, but she had turned the corner and her imagination had led the way.

Sometimes the difficulty does not lie in a given situation alone, but within the person. Experience may teach and the lesson, once learned, may be virtually impervious to change. It is an intriguing wonder of human beings that once we reach a conclusion, we resist changing, even when the evidence no longer supports the conclusion. This is nowhere more toxic than in a negative conclusion about the self. When you see yourself as unworthy, the number and power of your enemies will not matter; they are always strengthened by one. In your camp, there is always a spy to give away your position, your defenses, your weaknesses. There is always one to sabotage your strength, to take away your advantage, to betray any gain. Who is this enemy? It is you.

In assessing themselves, some have determined they are unworthy. In the absence of positive value, some have concluded that worthless equals vile; and as each of us knows, the wicked should be punished. At least, some part of the self seeks to punish another part of the self. Therein lies the hope. It is in the partition of doubt that psychotherapy for the self may take place.

It is an extraordinarily uncommon person in whom the assessment of the self is wholly in one camp or the other. No matter how positively we might view ourselves, there always remains some element of doubt. It is just so with the negative. In the depths of despair, in the equation of insignificance, there remains some element of positive self-worth, some pocket of resistance against the tyranny of self-derision. Psychotherapy is the process of developing that constructive force, of fanning the spark into flame, no matter how faint it may seem.

Here is how it went for one person. As he discussed his life and reactions to it, I saw that he was often the agent of his own destruction. His self-assessments cracked like the snap of a whip as he degraded any achievement and ridiculed his efforts as insignificant.

Nothing was sufficient to please his demanding inner critic. What to do? It seemed necessary to communicate with this demanding inner critic, but how does one converse with an attitude? One does it in the imagination.

I instructed him, "Close your eyes, and however you do it, search your mind; search yourself until you are able to locate and be in touch with that part of yourself that is so demanding, that critical part, that perfectionistic part of yourself." In that search of self-discovery, he found and named "Big Black." Big Black was, as you might surmise, condemning and judgmental. A stern, harsh, and unforgiving detractor, bereft of joy and pleasure. No effort, no achievement, no accomplishment was sufficient to please it.

You may be aware of aspects of yourself that seem to conform to this description. It is a part of most of us. In some, it comes to dominate. Such was his case. Big Black's understanding was that the man was lazy, unmotivated, and adrift; without Big Black's persistence and criticism, he would amount to nothing.

After our conversation with Big Black, I suggested that the man make contact with another part of himself, the part that was positive. He protested that there was no such part. Big Black was all there was. When one part is dominant, people often think it is everything. They have lost perspective on themselves and in their pain have failed to acknowledge the presence, even of the possibility, of a countering force within themselves. Consider, however, that if there is a critic, there must also be an actor, an artist, a player whose performance is criticized. For there to be criticism, there must be some action for the critic to evaluate. If there is a critic, possibly there is also an advocate.

So I said, "Now, close your eyes and make contact with that part of you that acts, that tries, that continues to strive in spite of the knowledge that it is going to be severely criticized no matter what it does." In this further journey of self-discovery, he found and named "Little Red." In these descriptions of Big Black and Little Red, he discovered dominance and proportion. He also discovered that while Big Black was big and dominant, Little Red was small in stature, but he was not insignificant and he did not lack for courage.

This can be a life-changing discovery. Ponder it for a moment. What does it mean to uncover within yourself an attitude that no matter what, no matter the odds, no matter the costs, you are worthy of great sacrifice? Metaphorically, there is a champion who will take up your cause time after time, and in spite of repeated defeat, will answer the call to fight on your behalf. If we can in some way offer assistance to the champion, we will do it. It was in this direction that this person went. He asked himself what help he could give to Little Red. In his conversation with Little Red, he discovered that the mere recognition of its existence was supportive and encouraging. Little Red had acted so long in anonymity that acknowledgment alone strengthened its determination. Appreciation empowered it even more.

This was not the end of psychotherapy. It was a significant beginning. Through time, the relative positions of Big Black and Little Red shifted in much the fashion of sand within an hour glass. The shift was not dramatic, but it was steady and incontrovertible. They became Big Red and Little Black. In the negotiations between these aspects of the self, we determined that Little Black had a role to play and did not have to be eliminated from the person's psychological structure. Its role changed and became less fanatical—often the resolution when perfectionistic parts of the self are confronted. Big Red, as the metaphor for positive self-worth, assumed its necessary dominant place, as is strategic in any healthy psychological structure. The promise is that these attitudinal, imaginary alterations will ripple through the intrapersonal, interpersonal, social, vocational, and behavioral dimensions of people's lives.

"The one thing I cannot do is take a bubble bath." What a poignant self-description of a person who is dedicated to giving to others. It represented for her the ultimate indulgence—selfish, unnecessary, wasteful, and decadent. She had taken on the responsibility for the care of others. She was the one to whom others turned in their times of need. For this person, such caretaking centered on her family, but in truth, it was a metaphor for her life. She would sacrifice for strangers if they asked. Giving was her way of life. What intervention is there for such self-sacrificing people?

Certainly, it does not lie in seeking to convince them that a giving way of life is inappropriate. Too many among us, it would seem, do not see the value of nurturing others.

This is a problem of amplitude, of a positive value vibrating too intensely. It is a problem of giving without receiving. There once was a vast sea that supported thousands of communities and millions of creatures, large and small. It gave each one nurture, sustenance, and sanctuary. In the course of time, the sea was cut off from the greater ocean and no longer sustained itself by the resources of the whole. Separated, isolated, and unnurtured, it continued to support those communities and creatures. It gave and gave and gave until it had no more to give. The name of that great inland sea is now Death Valley. Help ends when the helper is not sustained and nurtured.

Giving is a positive value. Many in our world fail to recognize that receiving is an equally positive value. How does one come to a balance between giving and receiving? People who are self-sacrificing cannot just be instructed or told. One way to get their attention is to shift the focus and make them the recipients of their own giving nature. There is a story about a self-sacrificing philanthropist who wanted a friend to select a person to whom all his worldly possessions would be given. When the word spread that someone would receive a gift of great wealth, hundreds of people showed up—the needy and the greedy, the worthy and the corrupt. The task was burdensome and unnerving. At last, the friend made his decision. He spoke to the philanthropist and said, "You have asked me to find the most giving and selfless person here to receive this gift. I have found him, and so I give it to you."

This a good story, and one that can be used in psychotherapy. A person might not be able to receive the gift. In psychotherapy, what can be done with a person who cannot take a bubble bath. What can be done for someone who is overly responsible for others? Imagination can play a part again.

"Take a moment and however you want to do it, imagine the list of people you are responsible for helping. The people you have to care about. See the list and tell me the names of the people on the list." Often, when the person recounts the names, his or her name is not on the list. "And now, imagine the list again. I want you to add your name to the list. And when it comes time to take care of the people you love, remember that your name is on the list. As you make your way down the list, you will come to you. Take care of you just as you take care of the other people on the list. You don't have to be first. You just have to be on the list." For such people, we can use their own goodness to be of help to them.

Somewhere between birth and young adulthood, all of us are expected to take control of our own lives. We are expected to become the pilot, guided by an inner compass and gyroscope. For some, expectation and achievement may remain unacquainted with one another. For some, the path of life is so well marked that they are fine simply following well-defined avenues. Later in life, some may lose their way and search for a new path with no notion of blazing one of their own. Others, ill-prepared for life by circumstances, become no more than game pieces pushed from experience to experience seemingly by the roll of a die or a spinning arrow. For whatever reason, some of us are, to paraphrase a line of poetry, neither masters of our fates nor captains of our souls. The control that does exist for such people lies in the hands of others. Such a state becomes a problem when one of three things happens; the path runs out, the controller leaves, or the "controlled" self rebels. When that happens, rudderless people may drift into psychotherapy.

Who should be in control of a person's life? Who should be at the center? For many, this is a philosophical, theological, and/or moral question that is worthy of discussions that far exceed the limitations of this small volume. For a psychotherapist, that control rightly belongs to the person seeking help. Clearly, the control being analyzed here is control for the self, not control over others. It is control of feelings, emotions, attitudes, and behavior. It is not control of circumstances. We may not control the elements, situations, people, and events of our lives, but we can control our response to these externals. We may need an inner journey, a journey into the imagination, to find the center, the sources of control.

What follows is an account of one such inner journey. There have been many that were individual and vivid, each dealing with

67

the unique demands of control needed for that person's life. The journey begins with a simple instruction.

Psychotherapist: I want you to search your inner mind for that place within you that might be called your center of control. It is a place deep within from which messages are sent that tell you how to react, how to feel, how to respond. You may close your eyes or not, and however you search is perfectly all right. As you search, tell me what you see.

Client: I am walking and it looks like a meadow. Yes, it is a meadow with grass and flowers and a stream flowing though the middle. I see a path and it is leading up to a house at one end of the meadow. I see the house now. Oh, it is run-down. The paint is peeling. The fence needs mending and the porch is falling down. The door is broken or off its hinges.

Psychotherapist: And what is this house? What is its meaning?

Client: It is my House of Control. This is my control center.

Psychotherapist: I see. Before you go any further, I want you to do whatever you have to do to repair the house. Clean up. Paint up. Fix up. Do that now and tell me what you see.

Client: First, I am fixing the fence. It is a picket fence. And now I am painting it white. Now I am fixing the porch and painting the house. Now I am repairing the door and all the windows.

Psychotherapist: Is it finished?

Client: Yes.

Psychotherapist: Tell me how it looks.

Client: Oh, it is beautiful. It is just the house I imagine that should sit at the end of a beautiful meadow. A lovely little cottage.

Psychotherapist: And now go inside and tell me what you see.

Client: I am going through the door and the inside is all messed up too. It is all dirty and shabby.

Psychotherapist: Fix the inside just as you have done to the outside.

Client: Okay, now it is pretty. Clean and light. Comfortable looking.

Psychotherapist: As you look at this comfortable place, I want you to locate the center. I don't know where it will be but it might be a separate room. Do you see it?

Client: Yes.

Psychotherapist: Tell me what you see.

Client: It is a little room. It has a broken door; inside, the room is dark.

Psychotherapist: Turn on a light and tell me what you see.

Client: It is dirty and has cobwebs. It looks like no one has been in here in years.

Psychotherapist: Somewhere in that little room there is some method of sending out messages to yourself. Do you see it? When you do, tell me what you see.

Client: Yes, it looks like big levers, the way I imagine how they used to change tracks for trains. I can't move them. They are rusty and stuck.

Psychotherapist: Now, just as you have repaired the outside of the house and cleaned up the inside, I want you to clean up and repair this control center. Do whatever you have to do to make it comfortable, warm, light, and functional. Shine and polish the levers, oil them, and do what you want to do so that the room is just as you want it to be. Tell me when you are finished and describe it to me.

Client: I am cleaning and polishing. The levers are chrome and shiny. There is a rug and a chair. I have some plants. It really is a comfortable-looking little room.

Psychotherapist: Good. Now look at the levers. I don't know how many of them there are or just how they work, but they might have labels and they might have numbers or indicators beside them. Perhaps, low to high or one to ten. Tell me what you see.

Client: It just says low to high.

Psychotherapist: Good. And now, one of those levers will have a

69

label on it. It will say something like "sticking up for myself" or "assertiveness." Do you see it?

Client:　Yes.

Psychotherapist:　What is the position of that lever now?

Client:　It is really low.

Psychotherapist:　I want you to move the levers up just a bit. It doesn't have to go all the way to high, but move it up just a bit.

Client:　Okay, I am moving it. Oh, it's easy. The oil is working.

Psychotherapist:　Good. And now the message has been sent. "Sticking up for yourself" is at a higher point than it was before. Now it is time to leave the control center. You know that you can come back to it any time you like. You know the way now. Before you leave, look at the door. You know how at the supermarket there will be a photograph of the "Manager on Duty"? Just to the right or left of the door there is a picture. Whose picture is it?

Client:　It is my mother.

Psychotherapist:　Now take your mother's picture out and in its place put your photograph—your photograph, and beneath it reads "Person in Charge." Do you see it?

Client:　Yes.

Psychotherapist:　Now close the door behind you and lock it in such a way that only you can open the door. This is your control center and only you may enter. Now come back to this room when you are ready.

What a dramatic and creative portrait of the self! A ramshackle old house with broken doors and rusted levers as a metaphor for a sense of control. In the imagination, the person has been able to repair the house, create an environment of comfort, and establish the mechanics of control. What this reveals is both the desire and the capability for control. Change is already beginning to take place. Just as in any psychotherapeutic change, the process has to move from the counseling room into the person's life. This guided trip into the imagination can be a first step in change.

Whether the issue begins in the disturbed sleep of a little boy, the violation of one person by another, crippling self-doubt, or the lack of self-control, the mind can imagine a solution. What the mind can imagine may not always come to pass, but it seems likely that what cannot be imagined will not be realized. The creative solutions of fantasy may well lead to the practical resolution of intensely felt emotional problems.

12

Wounded Healers

*P*sychotherapy is a profession plagued by myths. The myths surrounding the psychological health of psychotherapists are a study in polemics. The myths of the emotional health of psychotherapists range from "crazy" to "perfect."

Thomas Maeder examines the first myth in an article that opens with the teaser headline, "The helping professions, notably psychotherapy...appear to attract more than their share of the emotionally unstable."[1] The article, which I invite you to read, provides a number of anecdotal accounts of the "craziness" of psychiatrists, psychologists, and social workers. The professional literature is inconclusive on the emotional state of psychotherapists compared to other professionals, but the myth of the crazy psychotherapist is one that is frequently repeated. Newspapers apparently delight in reporting the clay feet of psychotherapists and any scandal, shortcoming, or misdeed is published with a nearly detectable clucking of the tongue. Perhaps that is as it should be. There may well be special obligations for those with special privileges.

Psychotherapists themselves are not immune from back-fence gossiping, and a social gathering of psychotherapists is likely to buzz in some private corner of the party with rumors of the moral and ethical lapses of colleagues. As Maeder says, "Psychiatrists often say that analysts are crazy. Analysts say that psychiatrists...are crazy. Both of them say that social workers and psychologists...are crazy. Not to be outdone, social workers and psychologists accuse psychiatrists and analysts, not only of being crazy, but pompous as well."[2] Some of this is petty. Some amusing. Some is serious. It is revealing of both the myth and facts of drug abuse and suicide among psychotherapists. For some, psychotherapy is a dangerous profession. Some may enter the profession already less than whole. Some may be overwhelmed by the profession, and each of us may know of some psychotherapist whose hold on emotional stability has become slippery.

At the opposite end of the continuum, there is the myth that psychotherapists are emotionally unflappable, invulnerable, and whole. The myth stems from a false and limited perception of psychotherapists seen only at work. A part of the training of psychotherapists involves the appearance of unflappability. This gets a bit complex, but it runs like this. The research and experience of psychotherapists over the years has affirmed and reaffirmed the concept of genuineness as an important dynamic of effective psychotherapy. An effective psychotherapist is not a phony. Still, such genuineness has to be "therapeutic." In each response they give, psychotherapists have to make a judgment about whether a particular intervention is therapeutic or not. Is the response both genuine and therapeutic? Thus, from the many responses and interventions open at any given moment in psychotherapy, some internal selection must be made.

Take a situation in which a person reports something that may be shocking, titillating, or even perverse. If we take an extreme example, a professional might be working with criminals. A murderer might report a particularly gruesome murder graphically and in appalling detail. Perhaps, the murderer eats part of the victim. On the inside, the psychotherapist might be thinking, "Wow, this is really strange," and, in fact, it is outside the range of ordinary, understandable human behavior. Psychotherapists, however, are trained not to respond with the ordinary and typical responses one might expect. Instead, one might see a calm and collected response. The psychotherapist might say, "So even though most people see that as shocking and perverse, the way you see it is the way anthropologists have described some hunters eating the liver of their prey? You gain power that way." It is a response that asks, "Am I understanding you correctly?" Of course, most psychotherapists would not encounter such graphic and shocking behavior in their clients. Nevertheless, the principle remains and we must face the reality that there is much that is shocking in our world.

One of the primary purposes of psychotherapy is to understand. It is sometimes difficult for many in our society to understand that the purpose doesn't change in psychotherapy even when the subject is a criminal accused and/or convicted of vile acts. In more sympathetic but equally dramatic situations, such a calm and understanding response can allow people to feel more hopeful and less victimized. Understanding is aided when therapists suspend judgment and resist moralizing. Suspending judgment can give the appearance of unflappability and lead people to think that, even in the face of what they consider to be their most shameful behavior, psychotherapists are such wonderfully understanding and noncondemning people that they must be perfect: the pinnacles of humanity; saints; people without problems. Psychotherapists put themselves in much danger, of course, when they start to believe this themselves.

There is yet a third myth—the myth of perfection, or the unsuitability of the less-than-perfect or wounded healer. Some might believe that anyone who has suffered some physical or psychological injury cannot be a psychotherapist.

Others hold a diametrically opposing view. Some believe that only those who have suffered can understand the suffering of another. The most provocative statement would be that only one who has suffered a particular shock should treat those who have experienced a similar trauma. One might find an advocate who argues, for example, that only combat veterans should do psychotherapy with other combat veterans. Another might argue that only recovering alcoholics should treat alcoholics. Another form of the argument is that one must come from some particular group to understand members of that group. Some insist, for example, that only homosexuals can understand and provide psychotherapy for a gay or lesbian person. Still others contend that culture is of such importance that only a psychotherapist who is Black, Asian, Hispanic, or Native American can understand someone fitting those descriptors. Some feminist thinkers assert that males cannot understand and therefore should not be psychotherapists for women.

Each of these beliefs is a myth. Each is wrong. Being an effective psychotherapist does not depend on leading a blameless or trauma-free life. Understanding does not depend on having experienced a particular form of suffering or belonging to some specific demographic group. Here is the dilemma. Each of these myths holds within it a small portion of validity. Some psychotherapists have been, and I presume some are, diagnostically disturbed. In fact, some of the most famous psychotherapists have experienced psychological disturbances as serious and debilitating as schizophrenia. Further, while psychotherapists need not be perfect or blameless, they do need to be sufficiently free of damaging psychopathology or present personal problems that they can understand and be of service to others. Also, it is not necessary to have suffered some emotionally damaging episode in life or to identify with a certain group to understand what others have gone through or are going through, but it may help.

Let's take the example of a psychotherapist who comes from a psychologically healthy environment and who has led a life of relative security. He experienced no abuse as a child or an adult; has not been victimized by violence or drugs; has maintained a stable marriage; and has experienced death only in its normal, natural, and expected role in life—the death of grandparents and/or parents at the end of their lives. How can such a person understand battering, incest, rape, war, or other life-disrupting incidents that hamper a person's effective living?

The question itself is formed in a misconception. First, the perception of the problemless life is false. All of us face difficult issues, problems, and dilemmas throughout our lives. We may see people who appear to have good lives and conclude that they do not have problems. Perhaps they are people who cope effectively. Perhaps our judgment is based on appearance and we fail to see the internal struggle. Whatever the case, each of us has faced personal crises. Each of us has enough tragedy in our lives to be able to understand the pain of others. What precedes understanding is the willingness and the compassion to expend the effort to understand. True, human tragedy is not meted out in equal measure. Some are blessedly spared from ravaging anguish and sorrow. Some are not, and they may become bitter and devastated.

I can understand the pain of a father whose son has died because I know how deeply I love my sons. We can understand other people through at least two different routes. One is the way of personal experience. I can understand because I have lived the experience. Experience alone, however, necessarily limits understanding. Each of us does not, and cannot, experience the whole of human endeavor. I do not, and cannot, experience the range of human thought, emotion, and behavior from zenith to nadir.

The other route to understanding is by seeking knowledge of the human condition. I can be taught, in psychotherapy itself, by people who confide in me and share their experience with me. I can read the accounts of those who tell others of their experiences, pains, and coping strategies. I can read works of other psychotherapists as they seek to tell us of their struggles to understand and work with people with damaging life experiences. I can immerse myself in the study of human experience and by so doing, come to understand what I have not experienced. I do not mean to imply that study and experience are the same; I do not mean that understanding and emotion are the same. I mean only that by study I can comprehend the meaning and importance of the experience for the person. It is a false belief that any human being can do more than that. Even those of us who have lived through the same experience bring to it our uniqueness. We are left to explore with one another how closely our experiences correspond. Our shared experience still demands our understanding and the comprehension of our unique meanings.

Sometimes we are cut; our wounds are deep and jagged. They leave scars. Some people prosper in spite of their scars. Ernest Hemingway is given credit for having said that we are strongest in our broken places,[3] and Nietzsche thought that what does not kill a person makes that person stronger.

This brings us to the concept of the wounded healer, one who has been emotionally injured and has turned to help others similarly injured. These people use their own experience of psychological trauma to be of service to others. The important principle is not the wound, however, but survival. Note that most people do not seek the help of a psychotherapist because of the background of the therapist. What they are seeking is knowledge, competence, and understanding to bring their lives to a place where they can live with themselves. Surviving psychological trauma alone is not sufficient. Saint Augustine resisted his own flaws, fought with his perceived faults, and, in the struggle, sought to find his own compassion, kindness, and mercy. Many of us know the tragedy of the cycle of battering, abuse, and incest. Perpetrators are often victims and victims become perpetrators. It is a vicious cycle and reveals the inadequacy of survival alone.

A therapist who has been hurt in some way needs survival that does not result in callousness, cynicism, or cruelty. For such therapists, painful emotional trauma, at sometime in their lives, has been followed by painful personal healing. From their own personal experiences and their ultimate resolution, these individuals have arrived at feelings of compassion for people who, like themselves, have had their lives battered by inhumane, dreadful treatment or its damaging opposite, emotional indifference. Their compassion becomes the starting place for the study and development of skills that will let them be of service to others. These qualities are represented in self-help support groups such as Alcoholics Anonymous, Compassionate Friends (support groups for parents whose children have died), Heartbeat (a support group for the surviving family members of suicide victims), SHARE (a support group for parents whose infants have died), or CanSupport (for persons diagnosed with cancer).

Sigmund Freud, no stranger to personal flaws, was a psychotherapist of remarkable courage. Maeder recalls Freud's "scrutiny of his deeply buried memories and then heroic confrontations with the painful things he found." Freud's willingness to search himself and then to "put his flaws at the service of the empathic process"[4] is the best and wisest use of hurt transformed into a healing capacity. The lie in the myth of the wounded healer is that the wounding is the significant element. It is not. Surviving in such a way that pain is transformed into compassion is the essential part. Someone has said that the best revenge is a good life—to survive, and out of the pain and a forecast of ruin, to construct a life of decency and strength. One form of the good life is to be of service to others.

13

The Problem of Power

*a*dvocacy is not dominion. Psychotherapy can be a siren whose song can lure the unaware and unprepared into appalling impropriety. The people who seek out psychotherapists are often vulnerable and see themselves as weak and unable to cope with their lives. In the psychotherapist, they seek a person who is calm, reasoned, and in control. Whether the psychotherapist is a pillar of strength or not, clients see an image of their own making and bring to this image various expectations. The skill of the psychotherapist is to make himself or herself clearly known so these expectations can be overcome. If a psychotherapist does not diligently strive for genuineness in the psychotherapeutic relationship, then he or she can easily fall prey to an illusion. The illusion is that the psychotherapist is responsible for healing the people who come for help.

Lynn Hoffman, a psychotherapist, stated the problem this way: "The illusion that one can unilaterally control other people underlies many problems that bring clients to therapy. My dilemma as a therapist is to free people from this illusion without buying into it myself."[1] Seduced by power, psychotherapists may become manipulative, exploitive demagogues. Psychotherapy may become a province in which the psychotherapist rules—a ruler in a domain where the ultimate failing of our profession is practiced with arrogant self-aggrandizement. The people who come for help have been diminished by such psychotherapists. They are less than they could be. Their ability to become autonomous human beings is usurped.

This is a considerable fault. The tantalizing mirage of power can corrupt many professions. Psychotherapy is no exception.

The perplexing thing about power in psychotherapy is that using it is not entirely wrong. My favorite story about power concerns Saul Alinsky, the social reformer and activist. He was once engaged to give a speech at a small college in the Midwest. Alinsky, a chain smoker, approached the podium to begin his speech with an ever-present cigarette hanging from his lip. The president of the college stood and informed Alinsky that smoking was not permitted in the auditorium. Alinsky looked the president squarely in the eye and said, "No smoking. No speech." The president sat down and Alinsky proceeded to give a speech on the uses of power![2]

Power may be used to teach, and it has its uses. The exercise of power is a delicate proposition and must be performed nimbly to avoid its many traps. One trap is the appearance that it is more useful than it really is. The uses of power are limited and yet we may believe that power is useful any time and anywhere; that all we need to do is try harder. Arthur Combs, an educator and psychotherapist, says there is nothing more dangerous than a partly right idea. People are not stupid. If something is wrong, clearly and definitively wrong, it will not work and people will abandon it; but if something works occasionally or to some extent, our solution is to try even harder. Because it seems to work a little bit, we might not ever stop trying to fix it. That is why a partly right idea is dangerous. It lures us into trying harder at something that isn't working optimally. We might pour good money after bad. If one glass of wine is relaxing, then a bottle will reduce stress entirely. In psychotherapy, if the people who seek my help see me as psychologically strong, as intellectually superior, as emotionally together, as socially insightful, perhaps I should give them the benefit of my perception. Surely, if they follow the recommendations of a person as clever as I, their lives will improve. Such is the temptation of flattery and power. The difficulty of psychotherapy is to avoid exploiting the vulnerability of clients in the name of helping them.

Genuine psychotherapeutic help is the certain movement in the direction of self-help. Anything that is done in psychotherapy that prevents this is false. It is false no matter how well intended the intervention. In the delicate use of power, a psychotherapist might well help a person develop his or her capacity for self-help. Just as in any other field of endeavor, power may be used or abused.

Power may be exercised in several different ways. Some are more helpful than others. One use of power is forbidden to psychotherapists. That is *power against*. It is the sort of power in which the aim is to diminish or harm. This is the abuse of power found in *One Flew over the Cuckoo's Nest*.[3] Nurse Rachett uses her power against a group of patients in a psychiatric hospital to crush their spirit. She becomes as powerful a force for psychopathology in the lives of these people as any in their experience. She is an active agent using her position, will, and personality to repress and devalue the people she is charged with helping. This dramatic fictional account, extreme as it is, pales before any actual account in which a psychotherapist has used his or her power against people. It pales, because it is fiction, in the face of genuine harm. Whether the exercise of power involves sex, religion, money, or submission, using it against clients in psychotherapy is without redeeming value.

Power may be of use in psychotherapy. A psychotherapist may have the *power to* gain access to services otherwise restricted to the client. This can be straightforward and simple. A physician may not have appointments available unless someone is referred. For a therapist to use his or her influence to secure an appointment for a client is appropriate. Using power to intervene between people and institutions, agencies, and other powerful individuals is proper and helpful. A man came to psychotherapy because of pain he was suffering after an implant operation. He had spoken to his surgeon and was assured that the pain was a normal part of the healing process and that perhaps seeing a psychotherapist could be helpful. The implication, of course, was that the pain was in his head and not in his groin. He could not get an appointment with his physician, who assumed, somewhat arrogantly, that the operation was a success and there were no complications.

After listening to the man's complaints, the psychotherapist called the surgeon. He suggested that although psychological issues might be involved, there could be physical ones as well, that perhaps, while attending to the psychological issues, it might be wise to do a more thorough physical examination. You know where this story is going, of course. The physical examination did reveal some complication and the implant was replaced. The pain subsided and the psychotherapy consisted of listening and using *power to* obtain an appointment and more than a hurried examination. This sort of power is helpful. It empowers people. It reassures them that they are in touch with reality, that their pains are not illusionary, that concrete steps can be taken to end their suffering.

In training, psychotherapists are cautioned again and again not to abuse power. Equally important for them to learn is the value of using *power for* people. People come to psychotherapists because they believe we have the competence, skill, and knowledge to help them. This is the authority of knowledge. This is the power of skill. We are expected to use this power in the service of the person seeking help. We convey this strength through assurance and straightforwardness. For example, if the therapist believes it is therapeutic to use a technique or counseling strategy, then a short declarative sentence is appropriate. "You said, 'I know I can do it.' Say it again.... And again, with even more conviction." This is using *power for* the person. It is reaffirming a felt sense of internal strength.

A psychotherapist might say, "Let's take some time in the session today to talk to your boss. Let's bring your boss into the session. Have him sit in this chair. Say, 'Boss, I have something I want to say to you.'" These directions are clear and direct. It is not directive. That is, it is not taking the issue away from the person and it is not creating an issue for the person. Instead, the psychotherapist deals directly with an issue the person has identified. This is an important distinction.

The psychotherapist may give homework. "I want you to write down the angry thoughts you have and when and what caused them. Record them and bring them with you to the next session. We will talk about them then." Because the person believes in the authority of the psychotherapist, he or she will do what is asked. Sometimes, a person does not, of course, but that becomes an issue of a different sort.

In therapy, a person wants understanding, information, and solutions to problems. A psychotherapist can use power for change. A person with many acquaintances but few friends might be instructed to have coffee with at least two acquaintances during the week. By making contact, the opportunity for a friendship becomes possible through association. An angry person may be asked to keep a journal of his or her angry thoughts during the day. The journal begins the process of bringing the anger under control. Brought into awareness, recorded, and reported, the anger can be discussed concretely and specifically with respect to when and in what situations it comes. Tasks such as these will often be completed because people believe in the power/authority of the psychotherapist. The psychotherapist can be of help because power is used for the person.

Psychotherapists can use *power with* a person so that his or her fears and anxieties do not have to be faced alone. In fantasy or in fact, a psychotherapist can accompany a person in confronting those fears. People who are afraid of enclosed places can step into an elevator with their psychotherapist. They may go into their past and confront old anxieties, and they do not have to do it alone. They have someone to accompany them on their journey into their own fears. People can increase their own sense of power from the support they feel from the psychotherapist. There is a world of difference between confronting demons alone and confronting them with an ally. It is the difference between loneliness and companionship—between a line and a circle. A single line is vulnerable from every angle; a circle is protected from every side. It is the difference between being able to carry a burden and being weighed down by it. There is a saying that a burden shared is a burden halved.

Power with means that two people are stronger than one. What might be overwhelming for a person alone can be withstood with the support of another. The psychotherapist can say clearly and without reservation, "I will stay with you during your struggle. I will not waver, and I will not turn away. I will not abandon you. We can face this. We can endure this together." To use power with a person demands courage from the psychotherapist. This courage can help clients to use power for themselves.

Power in psychotherapy is a matter of influence used as an *advocate for the psychological self*. It does not mean necessarily that the specific goals or behaviors of a person are buttressed through the power of the psychotherapist. Let's argue in extremes for a moment. Say a person is so angry with a co-worker that he wants to just "knock his head clean off." Obviously, using the power of psychotherapy to help the person bash his co-worker would be a mistake. The correct use would be to hear, acknowledge, and accept the person's emotions and anger as genuine. Using power to influence means to address directly, if possible, the anger itself. It does not mean to honor the typical cultural or societal responses to anger. To be an advocate for the psychological self means to seek understanding and solutions that enlarge and empower the person. It means seeking solutions that will, when utilized, enable the person to feel pride, respect, and dignity. To be an advocate for the psychological self means helping clients see through solutions that may endanger themselves or others. To acknowledge anger does not mean to advocate violence. To be an advocate for the psychological self does not mean to endure mistreatment passively. It means to empower people creatively to discover within themselves the resources they need to cope effectively with the tumult of their lives.

14

On Pundits, Wizards, Priests, and Clerks

*W*hy is it so difficult to be simply and plainly who we are? This is a question with which all psychotherapists wrestle— from meeting the first client throughout their lives as professionals. It is often the very question many clients struggle with as well. What keeps us from showing others who we are? Resistance and the processes of defense are the explanations we have given for clients. We have been unwilling to use the same explanations when as psychotherapists we mask ourselves, yet this explanation may be the source of some common, and mistaken, roles psychotherapists adopt as we strive to be of service.

A cornerstone of effective psychotherapy is the ability of psychotherapists to present themselves without guile, disguise, or deception. Psychotherapists must enable clients to see them as persons without withholding the essence of the self. A profound and potent psychotherapist is one who is present in the relationship without reticence. As it is with empathy and respect, so it must be with genuineness. Each psychotherapist must be present in the encounter for exploration, understanding, and change to occur most effectively and permanently. Most psychotherapists manage the transition from perplexity to congruence, but some make common therapeutic mistakes that plague them throughout their practice. Often the struggle to come to terms with the rigors of psychotherapy results in common and identifiable roles. The trials of personal genuineness prove too much for some individuals and they adopt masks or roles through which some image of a psychotherapist is presented. These roles represent a fundamental loss of faith in people. Each, in its own way, separates the psychotherapist from the client. Each lessens the involvement, reduces the risks, and dilutes the experience of psychotherapy. In the common human struggle to discover and create who we are, those psychotherapists who hide themselves from their clients damage two lives: their own and the client's.

The Mask of the Pundit

One way some psychotherapists reduce involvement is to remain aloof from the relationship. They adopt the mask of the pundit. They might listen to the story with rapt attention. They might gather information. They might ask penetrating questions. When the listening, gathering, and questioning are completed, what is left to do? Well, they do what pundits do. They analyze. They conclude. They offer opinions.

This is the mistake some psychotherapists have made in the recovered memories controversy. They have listened to symptoms and arrived at a diagnosis. A short story might make the point. I live in an agricultural and ranching community. I once saw a man standing on the side of the road holding a bridle. As I passed, I realized that I didn't know whether he had found a bridle or lost a horse. Behavior is like that. Behavior has a thousand parents. It is a serious psychotherapeutic mistake to make a diagnosis based on symptoms alone, but because they are learned and possess the facts, pundits shift the focus of the psychotherapy from the person to the psychotherapist. The period of listening is over and now the issue belongs to the psychotherapist. The psychotherapist does the talking now. The psychotherapist explains the origins of the problem, what is going on inside the head of the person, how it may be illogical and irrational, and what to do about it. And in all of this, the pundit hasn't gotten dirty, hasn't become involved in the fray, hasn't understood in any profound and acute or, metaphorically, heartfelt way the life of the other person. It is an antiseptic, hygienic, and aloof approach to psychotherapy that protects the psychotherapist from emotional material that can be personally frightening. It is an approach that leaves out the emotional aspects of life's problems. It is dangerous because it may lead the client to believe that this asymmetrical explanation can provide authentic respite from life's predicaments.

A merely intellectual understanding may give the appearance of resolution. Sometimes antiseptic answers do resolve life issues, especially in those situations in which any answer will do, and particularly if given by someone considered an authority; but any resolution to life issues given in the absence of understanding can be helpful only by chance. Any psychotherapist who is aloof to the experience of persons stands little chance of genuine understanding.

The Mask of the Wizard

Wizards heal by magic. They see themselves as possessing unique qualities or knowledge that produce amazing and astounding cures that baffle the professional community. Their practice includes special methods, devices, formalities, or strategies that everyday practitioners have failed to discover or do not use because of "narrow-mindedness" or "scientific snobbishness." They may present themselves as gifted and blessed or as unrecognized geniuses. They may be charismatic and attract disciples through the sheer force of their personalities. They may invoke the power of the supernatural. They may imply the endorsement of science. In all this, magical psychotherapists are untouched by the human experience. The resolution to life's quandaries lies in some technique or technology, in the plea to a power outside the self, in the practice of some ritual, or in the surrender of the self to the power of the magician. Some people and some problems may be ameliorated by magic.

Perhaps, the most famous example of a "wizard" would be Anton Mesmer, the founder of *mesmerism*. Mesmer created a climate of mystery. He would dress in costume, surround people with paraphernalia, load them up with laxatives, sink them in warm water, create an atmosphere of the mysterious, and make a show of moving magnets around them. Many became hysterical, crying out as if in pain or in the throes of some powerful struggle. In this intense climate of suggestion, and in highly charged emotional states, illnesses disappeared, paralysis lifted, ailments vanished. Mesmer claimed that these cures were the result of an unrecognized force in the universe only he had discovered called *animal magnetism*. He controlled its forces and used its power for good—and profit. Ultimately discredited, animal magnetism took its place as one more human foible.[1]

Mesmer was not and is not alone in his perfidy. Charlatans throughout history have made their larcenous way by healing the unsick. They assign mysterious explanations to ordinary human experience. They take credit for the natural power of the body and of the mind and, in so doing, insult and demean people. They have betrayed their implied loyalty to their patrons. They are among the most reprehensible of psychotherapists.

The Mask of the Priest

In this section, I use *priest* in its metaphoric and disparaging form, as one who moralizes or makes sermons about some *a priori*, presupposed good. This person pontificates on the way it is supposed to be.

Most of the time we associate the word *priest* with religion, but there are preachers in the psychotherapy community, too, especially on the subject of self-help. Self-help is important and necessary, but it has also achieved a prominence in which the promise of simple answers and easy solutions has created a market for psychological priests. In this context, the solution is not necessarily a religious or spiritual good, but rather some assumption of psychological good. These *priests* provide formulas for living and ending suffering. They promise that those who are willing to follow the formula rigorously and faithfully will have the confusion and pain of life lifted from them. This involves a judgment that people are, in the main, unhealthy, in a state of iniquity, and in need of salvation and forgiveness. It embraces a venal and specious practice of psychotherapy.

This position is grounded on three errors. The first is arrogance. The second is distortion. The third is destructiveness.

The position of this type of priest is *arrogant* because the psychotherapists involved in such a practice have elevated themselves to a position of moral superiority. They have assumed for themselves alone the knowledge of what is righteous and orthodox. It is arrogant because the psychotherapist has made himself or herself a teacher of righteousness.

Assuming such a position is a *distortion* because it asks people to learn or be taught directly to think in particular ways, adjust their bodies, eat certain foods, reflect in a disciplined fashion, and/or behave in prescribed ways. In all this, the power is presumed to lie in the method or practice, and the psychotherapist is the mentor/intermediary through whom the person must learn.

Let us be clear about this distortion. You can't hypnotize a rock because a rock does not have the capacity to benefit from the treatment. No matter how powerful we consider a treatment or how elegant the philosophy, the power to change lies in the person seeking change. This truth is fundamental in biology, in medicine, and in the environment. It is also fundamental in psychotherapy.

The *destructiveness* lies in the reasons people come to psychotherapy. They come because they have not learned or have lost touch with their own capacity to cope with the enigmas, quandaries, complications, and tragedies of life. They may be, and in all likelihood are, vulnerable and confused. They find reassurance in an opportunity to explore this vulnerability and confusion, to seek the source and reasons for them, and, ultimately, to discover what to do about them. The destructive element is the exploitation of this vulnerability in leading clients to solutions, philosophies, practices, and/or life decisions that are more important and central to the psychotherapist than to any self-discovered and self-initiated personal resolutions. These introjected outcomes weaken clients and prepare them poorly for their continuing life outside the confines of the psychotherapeutic relationship. To replace the turmoil of a person's life with some philosophy or system of behavior may help for a time—time enough to propagandize new converts—but experience has taught us that imposed and introjected systems deteriorate and the person is left with not only the continuing original turmoil but the crisis of new concerns over who may now be trusted as a source of help. One "psychological priest" can taint an entire profession.

There is, of course, a place for judging or moralizing, a time for the consideration of moral philosophy, a time for evaluating right and wrong. Any person and any society must make moral decisions. Psychotherapy is both a process and a time in which persons can and do make moral decisions. They do so with the assistance, and perhaps support, of a psychotherapist. Do not lose sight of the first three words in the preceding sentence. *"They* do it." Any psychotherapist who presumes to make decisions for others distorts the purpose of psychotherapy.

The Mask of the Clerk

A clerk is one who takes information, keeps records, tabulates, writes reports, and so on. In psychotherapy, these practices may take the form of testing, assessment, and diagnosis. These processes represent a part of the psychotherapeutic enterprise, but doing only these would be analogous in medicine to completing an examination, blood tests, and analyses, concluding that the patient has appendicitis, and doing nothing further. Such behavior is the pretense of care and the accomplishment of nothing.

There are times, however, when very little action seems to produce change. You might possibly run across someone who will tell you that in his practice some person was helped and all he did was give her some tests and provide the test results. It could happen; it does happen. The phenomenon is called the placebo effect. Psychological relief may come from the belief that one is receiving treatment even though no treatment is being given. Being placed on a waiting list for treatment, for example, has triggered a sense of relief in certain patients. It is the belief that is creating the relief. There is no great harm in this phenomenon unless a psychotherapist consciously uses it to manipulate people.

Now, back to the mask of the clerk. The purpose of assessment and diagnosis is to inform the psychotherapy. They are not psychotherapy itself. Psychotherapists who stop at these procedures are uninvolved in the lives and understandings of the people they have sworn to serve. Just as surely as testing, assessment, and diagnosis are meant to inform psychotherapy, psychotherapy can inform testing, assessment, and diagnosis. In plain fact, to separate one from the other represents yet another distortion of the psychotherapeutic process. To believe that people may be understood through the application of testing procedures alone slights and degrades human experience. Psychotherapy is not a process of external observation, evaluation, interpretation, and explanation. It is not an impersonal endeavor. It is subjective in the sense that to comprehend another person, the psychotherapist must understand the meanings that person gives to his or her answers and behavior in any assessment. To do otherwise confuses appearance with substance. This is the mistake of the clerk.

The Roleless Role

If psychotherapists are not pundits, wizards, priests, or clerks, then who or what are they? The problem in each of the roles above is that each *is* a role; and when psychotherapists mask themselves, they prevent a genuine relationship from forming. The role of a psychotherapist is to have no role. At the expense of sounding like a Zen philosopher, the phrase means to be truly who you are. To be your true self means to avoid phoniness and role playing. It means not presenting yourself as an *image* of a psychotherapist. It means presenting *who you are* as a psychotherapist.

Years ago, one of the dominant training principles and metaphors for psychotherapists was known as *suspension of the self*. In essence, it meant that psychotherapists were in the therapeutic relationship for the other person, that psychotherapists should not bring their personal issues into the session or introduce their personal lives into the psychotherapy. This practice even extended to how we dealt with a headache or a cold. We were instructed to leave the headache at the door. This approach implied a passive sort of psychotherapy in which the psychotherapist was wholly dedicated

93

to the needs of the client and kept his or her own person out of the room. I have, of course, stated this principle in its extreme to make the point.

Over the years, this concept gave way to another training metaphor labeled the *self as instrument* approach. For this, psychotherapists are taught to use their personal qualities as a vehicle to help others. If a psychotherapist is by nature quiet, the training task is to develop that tendency so that it serves the therapeutic relationship. If he or she is by nature active, the training task is to develop that tendency to serve a therapeutic purpose. With a dramatic nature, the psychotherapist would use more dramatic interventions to facilitate the relationship. This understanding of psychotherapy espouses no one proper way to enter the psychotherapeutic relationship. How an individual practices psychotherapy is, instead, a personal and unique process guided by research into effective psychotherapy and tempered by the therapist's individual qualities. In this chemistry of the common, blended with the unique, the personal qualities of the psychotherapist can be present in the therapeutic relationship as psychotherapeutic tools. Any role that hides the unique qualities of the psychotherapist—whether as pundit, wizard, priest, or clerk—does a disservice to the therapeutic relationship. Psychotherapists struggle through study and practice to present an undistorted image. In so doing, they free each client from a burden he or she did not bring to therapy. The client does not have to second guess the relationship with the psychotherapist. Other aspects of the client's life may be clouded, but the person of the psychotherapist, at least, will be clear.

15

On Giftedness, Intuition, and Sensitivity

*M*yths are insidious. They persist, sometimes in spite of solid evidence to the contrary. They may have their origins in some thread of truth, but myths are false beliefs. The danger of myths lies in the tendency of people often to be guided more in terms of their beliefs than by what they know.

One of the lingering and destructive myths that hangs on in the field of psychotherapy is the myth of giftedness. Newspaper articles, books, television, and the movies all labor diligently to perpetuate the myth of the gifted psychotherapist. Let's set the scene. The billionaire's son has endured some unnamed trauma. Perhaps he was captured in some far-off land and tortured by a previously unknown jungle tribe. After he is rescued, he is returned home only to face a life of mental torment. The anguished billionaire seeks the advice of his equally wealthy friend who tells him that years earlier his wife, whom everyone thought was on a world tour, was, in actuality, in treatment with a famous and brilliant psychotherapist. She has fully recovered because of the revolutionary treatment she received from the brilliant and extraordinarily gifted psychotherapist. You've heard this story. You may even have repeated it in one of its many versions. In less financially gifted families, a worried father may talk to his wife who recommends Aunt Mary. Aunt Mary is the recognized therapeutic relative. Others may endorse the family physician or the pastor, who have no more training in psychotherapy than Aunt Mary, but who do have distinct sets of myths and credentials surrounding them.

I am not trying to disparage Aunt Mary, physicians, or pastors. I also do not deny that there are people in the world who are helpful to many because they are compassionate. In their own life experiences they have learned to reserve judgment and not to leap readily to condemnation. Without arrogance, I say bless them and recognize the limits of their ability to help.

But consider this. You need legal help, so I recommend Aunt Mary because she is naturally gifted in the law! Or you have broken your leg, so I recommend an accountant I know because accountants are schooled and must know about healing, too. Uncle Jim is a gifted toothpuller. I am, of course, exaggerating and being foolish. Who believes any longer that physicians, attorneys, dentists, or accountants come by their skills and knowledge "naturally"? Some seem to believe that people trained in one field accrue the competencies of another through some automatic process, but this is not so.

Some people seem to believe, however, that there are those who have the skills and knowledge of psychotherapy naturally. For one reason or another, through belief in a gift of intuition or extraordinary sensitivity, some people decide they have the natural abilities that qualify them to be psychotherapists. They may believe they are more sensitive than others or may have been told by their friends that they seem to feel more deeply than others. They may believe they are more caring than others and therefore they can be of help. The myth is that understanding comes from sensitivity rather than training. Many people care; they simply do not know what to do. Consider the families and loved ones of any person who comes to psychotherapy. Should we conclude that they are insensitive and uncaring? More likely, they do care, but their ability to suggest solutions and resolutions has been exhausted and the troubled person is now seeking help outside the ordinary networks.

Some people believe they can know the inner motivations and concerns of others without the conscious use of reason. They might even succumb to the seductive notion that they are more knowledgeable of another person than the person himself or herself. They are gifted with intuition. Thus, they may prescribe courses of action to others. For psychotherapists to believe that they are some-

how able to sense what others are missing is arrogant and dangerous. It invites the misuse of power. It separates psychotherapists
from the common humanity they share with the persons who come
to them for help.

In one of its other manifestations, this myth of the naturally
gifted therapist takes the form of the "weekend wonder." In addition to believing themselves gifted with sensitivity or intuition, these
people believe another myth—that all they need in addition to their
natural intuition is the proper method. They know they lack training and skill, so off they go to weekend training workshops in Mental Somaticism or the Zauberhaft Method or Bilateral Neurodynamic
Cybernetics or some other academic or esoteric-sounding technique
professing to be psychotherapy. After a short period of instruction
and some form of certification, they set up practice using a title
that bypasses the laws governing the practice of psychotherapy.

Competent practitioners in any field of study struggle, practice, and refine their work, yet the belief endures that some natural ability, coupled with minimal training, qualifies one to be a psychotherapist. To hold that the weekend study of anything qualifies
one as competent in any field is a false and potentially dangerous
belief. The people who come for help in psychotherapy are vulnerable. They deserve a practitioner who has taken time for education
and training. There is honor in it. There is dishonor and potential
danger in the overvaluation of one's giftedness.

97

16

The Ethics of Psychotherapy

*E*thics is what you do, and put simply, you should do the right thing. But what is the right thing? Therein often lies the rub. Helping professionals have been let off the hook to some extent. We have agreed to abide by a set of guidelines voted on by the membership of the professional organization to which we belong. These codes of conduct provide professionals with minimum standards for governing their professional behavior.

In another part of this book, the importance of understanding, realness, and respect are discussed. Ethics is about *respect*. A professional code of ethics sets forth minimum standards of conduct for professional helpers in their relationships with one another, the public in general, and the people who come for help in particular. The best psychotherapy, of course, does not adhere to *minimum* standards alone, and the best psychotherapists need neither to be reminded nor compelled to do the right thing.

I want to stress the statement that opened this chapter: Ethics is about behavior. Ethics is about what we do. To believe that ethics is about thoughts or feelings is a serious and punishing mistake. We are not unethical because we have random, irrelevant thoughts or even feelings of sexual attraction; if this were the standard, few of us would remain as psychotherapists. Many of the people in psychotherapy come because they are incapacitated by their own thoughts. A part of our work is to help them realize that thoughts flow freely and there is no need to punish themselves merely because of their thoughts. This observation applies to psychotherapists as well. As psychotherapists, we must understand that random thoughts and wayward feelings come to us all and must be considered normal and without cause for concern. Fred Richards, a psychotherapist, says "The fantasy is not the act; the desire is not the deed."[1] Treated in such a fashion, aimless and haphazard thoughts merely pass through as we continue with our business of listening, attending, and helping.

What is ethics about? For psychotherapists, professional codes address a wide variety of concerns ranging from rules about how to handle paperwork to matters of principle and social responsibility. For psychotherapy specifically, our professional code calls us to behavior that is respectful, honest, private, skilled, and steadfast.

Respect lies at the heart of psychotherapy. Respect is demonstrated in two distinct ways. First, it is revealed in how we act toward the people who come for help. Take an old analogy about understanding hopefulness in people's lives. Look at a glass containing water. Is it half full or half empty?

If we see the glass as half empty, when people come for help, we may well view them as flawed individuals who need to be fixed. In this view, we see them as incapable of helping themselves and needing someone else to teach them, mold them, direct them, or correct them. This could be called a deficiency model.

The other view is that the glass is half full. With this view, we are likely to recognize the strengths, capabilities, knowledge, and competence of clients and help them to marshal their skills in dealing with the concerns that brought them to psychotherapy. This might be called the adequacy model.

There is yet a third alternative. Perhaps there is nothing at all wrong with the level of the water. The problem may be the size of the glass. In this view, people are seen as quite adequate, and whatever problems they are having lie outside themselves. They may still have problems of thought, but the source of the hurt and the etiology of the pain lie in circumstances outside their direct control. Their problem is in the environment that defines them. The most obvious illustration of this situation is oppression. Oppression may exist at home or at work, in one-to-one relationships, or in the culture. A wife may be emotionally tyrannized at home and conclude that the fault lies within herself. An employee might suffer the insults of an overbearing boss without recognizing that his perceived shortcomings are artifacts of the supervisor's constant criticism. Members of an ethnic or national minority may come to doubt their personal strengths in the face of constant ridicule. In each of these instances, the qualities of the person are not in need of psychotherapy; a change in the environment is the solution to the dilemmas. This approach might be called the radical model.

There is more to respect than recognizing competence. The second way to demonstrate respect is by a willingness to understand the client's point of view. Respect, for the psychotherapist, includes being nonjudgmental. At this point, some people balk at the psychotherapeutic process, arguing that certain behavior is so contemptible it cannot be tolerated. They misunderstand psychotherapy. To be respectful, to respond nonjudgmentally, and to strive for understanding do not represent approval or agreement. In their private lives, psychotherapists hold a wide variety of personal values. Psychotherapists may be involved in political parties, religious organizations, and/or social reform movements. They may hold deeply rooted values and have personally strict moral codes. Professionally, however, they have agreed to suspend their personal views, no matter how deeply felt, in favor of a professional value system that emphasizes understanding and respect.

An important point to explore here is how a person who has a strong value is able to resist introducing or even forcing that value on a client who is obviously violating it. Such client behavior can range from the dramatic and reprehensible to the ordinary and banal, from battering to sexual experimentation. With a client who is acting out values that contradict the personally held values of the psychotherapist, how can the therapist remain honest, congruent, and respectful? The answer lies in another value. An example from an entirely different profession can illustrate. Professional soldiers might be forced to act in ways that severely contradict their personal values. In a specific situation—training or actual combat—soldiers are called on to perform duties that in another situation would be totally unacceptable. A less dramatic situation could be played out on the athletic field. A high school wrestler might have to inflict pain on an opponent in the contest to win the match. The wrestler could conceivably be a gentle soul who would not think of physically hurting another person in daily life. Something of the sort happens in psychotherapy. Just as high school wrestlers or professional soldiers operate on a different value system to accomplish their ends, psychotherapists operate on a system that values respect of persons and understanding of behavior. That is the therapeutic task.

Another aspect of ethics is *honesty*. Like respect, honesty has at least two meanings. One is straightforward honesty. Psychotherapists mean what they say and say what they mean. They don't lie, cheat, or steal from clients. Beyond this businesslike approach is a second, more profound meaning of honesty in a psychotherapist. A psychotherapist is expected to be transparent. The importance of nonjudgmental respect, discussed earlier, includes the idea of suspending personal values for a professional value that has demonstrated itself to be helpful: the creation of a climate of understanding, respect, and genuineness. But how can a psychotherapist be genuine if he or she has a value that is different from the client's? My answer is my honest belief that empathic understanding and respect from the therapist are the best ways to help a client achieve a personality change, if that is what is needed. Others therapists view the transparency called for in psychotherapy as therapeutic transparency or therapeutic genuineness. What part of the psychotherapist's experience, if revealed, will be therapeutically helpful for the client? We don't just tell clients about our personal lives, we make professional judgments about whether some personal view or experience can be helpful to them. These decisions will involve revealing some aspect or experience as well as keeping others back. Both decisions are honest.

Psychotherapists are not gossips. What is said between a client and a psychotherapist is personal, private, and unrevealed. This confidentiality paves the way to trust. Obviously, people in therapy reveal information that is sensitive, delicate, and possibly embarrassing. For them to risk bringing their fears and vulnerabilities into the open, they must know that what they say is *private*. Psychotherapists ethically must not talk in any specific way about the clients they see. They will, of course, talk about situations that happen in therapy, just as I have in this book, to make a point or teach some principle of psychotherapy; but the particular clients must be unrecognizable—sometimes even to themselves. In this climate of privacy, sufficient trust is built for a person to come to understand his or her own worst fears and begin the sure movement toward solutions or outcomes that are effective and lasting.

An important point is that the privacy of psychotherapy is not absolute. As a part of honesty, clients must be told from the beginning that not everything said in psychotherapy is private. Children need to understand that their parents or guardians have a right to know what goes on in therapy. Court-ordered clients need to know that the court will have access to what happens in therapy. Even more important, clients must know that the target of any violent threat will be warned. Often, people seem to reveal their violent thoughts or suicidal plans with the hope that someone will intervene and stop them. Psychotherapists can be relied on to do something to protect the people who may be harmed. Children must be protected; if there is any hint of abuse, it must be examined and, if necessary, reported. Sometimes clients react with anger and reject the psychotherapist because he or she took steps to protect either the client or another person. Know that life is more important than a therapeutic relationship. In any case of the possibility of physical harm, err on the side of caution and act to protect the endangered one.

103

Psychotherapists do not practice by trial and error. They are *skilled* and do what they know how to do. They do not try to work with issues they are not trained to handle. Part of the trust necessary for psychotherapy to advance is clients' conviction that the psychotherapist can understand and help them. This faith in the psychotherapist's skills contributes to client trust.

The implication here is not that a therapist needs direct experience to be effective. Psychotherapists need not have been suicidal to understand the hopelessness that can lead to self-destruction. They don't have to have been battered to understand the violation, the loss of trust, and the indecision of someone who has. Sometimes, having had experiences that approach those of clients can be helpful, but the important point is that the *client's* experience must be understood; possibly the psychotherapist's experiences are irrelevant to this client. To conclude hastily that we understand another simply because we share a common experience is a serious psychotherapeutic mistake. We may use our experience to check our understanding with the client's to see whether they are similar; if they are, our own feelings have served as a helpful guide. Even so, the most important quality in psychotherapy remains empathic skill, not shared experience.

Ethically, psychotherapists commit themselves to struggling with a client until the task is done. In this commitment, a psychotherapist is *steadfast.* As long as the client continues with the struggle, the psychotherapist will stay with that person. Psychotherapists do not abandon clients because the going gets rough. There are, of course, legitimate reasons for discontinuing therapy. If progress is stalled, a respite from sessions might help. If the client seems not to be profiting any longer, continuing is unreasonable. Sometimes, finances interfere with a client's ability to continue in therapy, but that alone is not a reason for discontinuing psychotherapy.

There is meaning in sticking with people. The idea of brilliant insights, dazzling interventions, and elegant solutions generally belongs to the realm of myth; successful outcomes in psychotherapy often come from staying with the tasks long enough to wear out defenses and push away confusion. Psychotherapy may well succeed more by determination and constancy than by penetrating insight of the therapist.

Ethics is what psychotherapists do. They are expected to demonstrate respect, act honestly, keep a client's personal life private, practice in those areas in which they are skilled, and stay with clients through difficult times. These behaviors capture the essence of ethical responsibility with clients. Other considerations could be listed, of course, and you should read and understand the ethical code you follow. Clearly, however, if you are respectful, honest, private, skilled, and steadfast, in all likelihood your practice of psychotherapy will be ethical and effective.

17

Paths of Diversity

*P*sychotherapy places an extremely high value on the uniqueness and worth of the individual. Each person presents himself or herself to the therapist in the richness and singularity of individual experience. Yet each of us, as unique and singular as we are, is a thread in a fabric. As we weave ourselves into life, we discover ourselves not only as single threads but as part of a pattern—a recognizable cloth that is sometimes as distinctive as the individuals who are its parts. We have woven ourselves into the family, culture, and religion of our experience. Perhaps, if we stopped there, we would be more understandable to one another. The process, however, continues and our single fabric of identifiable design becomes part of a quilt of mixed patterns, with threads of such variety as to challenge the most organized and seeking mind. Clearly, we are a diverse lot.

Our diversity follows two paths: One, that we are individuals, and two, that we are part of some larger whole. We are unique individuals born into families that are part of yet larger wholes. We are each tied into a culture, a religion, a nation. Each of us becomes identified with a gender role and, whether we like it or not, a racial category. Some of us find that even the more easily understood categories of human experience are not sufficient to contain the groups to which we freely identify ourselves or into which we find ourselves typed. We may be grouped because of our sexual orientation. We may be typed because of some physical disability. For whatever reasons, human beings seem to share an amazing capacity to group themselves and one another into an array of diverse categories.

Not surprisingly, the similarities we share with our identified group come to have as much meaning and importance for us as our uniqueness. Those similarities form a common bond that binds us together into recognizable wholes, whether those bonds are from kinship, physical traits, or some more abstract connection such as religion, language, culture, or sexual orientation. The relationship between our individual uniqueness and our connectedness is truly the metaphor of the candle flame and the impenetrable darkness. Who can say where the flame ends and the darkness begins? Who can say where our individuality ends and culture begins? Who can separate his or her individual being from the impact and socialization of gender? Who can pluck one person from the ethnic sea and expect that one to emerge dry and untouched by the waters of tradition and expectation?

Thus, we have these simultaneous truths: We are different from one another and we are like one another. For psychotherapists, the uniqueness of every client must be grasped. Every client must be understood, as well as possible, within the context of the great formative influences of life—biology, gender, race, ethnicity, culture and religion. We might say, flippantly, that we cannot understand fish if we do not understand water. We might also say, in all seriousness, that we cannot understand human beings if we do not understand diversity—individual and collective.

America is home to a bewildering array of differences. How can a professional helper cope with all the linguistic, ethnic, national, religious, socioeconomic, and value differences that clients present as they seek our help? We must never approach people as categories. With the great importance psychotherapy places on recognition of the uniqueness and worth of the individual, it is a terrible insult to individual worth for psychotherapists to treat people like stereotypes because of some assumed knowledge of their backgrounds and traditions. On the other hand, it is necessary and respectful for therapists to be knowledgeable of the identifiable patterns of experience people may bring with them as they seek our counsel. We are left with a question. How can we know the full array of diversity that surrounds us? We can't.

I said earlier that I live in a small town. Even so, as I write this chapter and look out my window, I see across the street the home of a housewife who was originally from Taiwan; just up the block lives a black man from Ghana; only a few houses to the right lives a Hispanic family. In between are other men and women, young and old, single, married, and divorced, with various religious beliefs. Even though we share a neighborhood, there is no guarantee that we share the same values. As helping professionals, psychotherapists know that anyone of that neighborhood could seek our help. How can I know beforehand which of the rich traditions that exist in any community an individual client will bring, or how significant the traditions will be in that client's life? As helping professionals, we should inform ourselves in many ways about the concerns that come with a diverse society; and we should also acknowledge that no one of us can possibly study, much less grasp, the range of diversity that is America. What shall we do?

The Path of Knowledge

I have an acquaintance who is a psychotherapist. She was telling me about a new client she was seeing—a family, in fact. They were from a far away place and from a culture very different from the dominant culture in the United States, also the background of the native-born psychotherapist. What she said was instructive. "When I knew I was going to see them, I went to the library." What a revealing statement! The psychotherapist did not know about the background, history, or culture of a family who had called to see her, so she began learning immediately. Some might fault her for not knowing. Some will understand that we cannot predict which person from what corner of the world might come to us. Whichever point of view we take, we can all honor the attitude of respect and care that was exhibited by this counselor and that we could hope for in ourselves. She did not have the information she needed, and she did what was necessary to find it. Her initial research may prove to be insufficient. If it is, however, we know that this helper will do what is necessary to learn about these particular clients.

I have another acquaintance who is a counselor for the Arapaho and Shoshone people on one of the reservations on the great Western plains. I was instructed by this psychotherapist as well. He lives in the community and knows that his clients will come from particular backgrounds. He also knows that the Arapaho and the Shoshone are not the same. One of the things he said to me was this: "I have an obligation to immerse myself in the community. I study and learn and talk to the people." He walks the path of respect as well. If we know we are going to be working with a particular culture, ethnic group, gender population, sexual orientation, religious point of view, or age group, as respectful helping professionals, we should enroll in classes, seek out experiences, and absorb everything we can of that experience to know, understand, and accept more respectfully the diversity the clients bring.

There are two paths to diversity. One is the common and knowable experiences shared by a group—sometimes a nation, sometimes a culture, sometimes a tradition, sometimes a religion, sometimes a practice. When that is the case, as helping professionals, we can do what is necessary to inform ourselves so as to facilitate our learning the other path.

The Path of Empathy

The other path to diversity is understanding the individual client in all his or her richness and uniqueness. As psychotherapists, we must recognize that regardless of background, the person who sits before us is a unique, self-aware, and conscious being. We must not be so informed about culture and other forms of diversity that we lose sight of the *individual* who has come to us for help. Whatever background we share—from dominant culture to the least represented minority—we are each different within our traditions. It is a mistake to assume that people from the same culture or group uniformly share the values of that tradition or group. The task of psychotherapists is to use our knowledge of clients' backgrounds as the beginning of insight while we remain open to the full personality of the one who has sought us.

The path of empathy often begins in self-examination, and by extension, in an examination of our own background and cultural beliefs. We need to understand ourselves and our own emergence from a dominant culture. Our particular background, economic past, and sociocultural traditions have provided each of us with strong images about our worth as persons, our position in the world, and our status relative to others. Without examining these issues, even well-meaning psychotherapists may not be able to see and hear what is necessary to understand other realities. This is the path of empathy.

A Note of Caution

We *are* a diverse lot. There is much difference among us. It is possible on inspection to understand and respect our differences. We can accept the reality of one another's view of the world. Many traditions have created many different practices. Many of these practices are good, many are harmless, and some are dangerous and hurtful. For the helping professional, acceptance does not imply agreement or approval. Respect does not overlook harm. There is danger for us as helping professionals if we become so relativistic as to see all practices as acceptable. We fail to maintain standards of practice if we see cultural difference as a justification for cruelty. In the world of the past, for example, foot binding may have pleased some aesthetic perspective, but it maimed generations of Chinese girls. In the modern world, genital mutilation is practiced under the defense that it is a cultural or religious practice that no one has the right to challenge. In psychotherapy, we fail to protect the welfare of the client if we permit abuse or neglect because of a client's claim of individual values or of religious practice. The helping professional has both a legal and an ethical duty to protect the physical and psychological welfare of the people who come to us for help. Regardless of our respect and knowledge, age, gender, sexual orientation, culture, ethnicity, nationality, religion, disabil-

109

ity, and/or socioeconomic class are not justification for anyone to harm another. The transcendent professional and ethical value is that, as helping professionals, above all, we do no harm; to the extent that it is possible, we permit no harm to or by clients. We are challenged to recognize and respect the diversity within which, individuals grow and develop. No helping professional should ignore, and thus demean by lack of attention, the defining categories of a person's life.

18

Issues, Problems, and Dilemmas

*a*s the bumper sticker warns us, "Shit Happens." However scatological and unfortunate this phrasing may be, it captures an unpleasant reality. Frederick (Fritz) Perls, a psychotherapist, theorist, and no stranger to scatological phrasing, further informed us that shit comes in three forms: chickenshit, bullshit, and elephant shit. We are facing two truths. Bad things happen, and some things are worse than others.

The experiences of life, both positive and negative, come by degrees. This book is concerned with the experiences that trouble and afflict us. There is, naturally, much in life that is joyful, constructive, positive, and affirming. These are matters that do not ordinarily call for the skills of psychotherapists.

Psychotherapists are asked to help people cope with the darker side of life. People come to a psychotherapist when they are hurt, confused, and disoriented, but they come after suffering different degrees of harm. Physically, a harmful experience may be something like a sunburn. A sunburn hurts, causes discomfort, and may disrupt our plans. The pain can be eased with ointments and sprays. Time, and some care, heals. In emotional terms, a sunburn might be labeled an *issue*. As with a sunburn, emotional issues are frequently of short duration and have a strong possibility of total healing. Issues are matters of concern in our lives. They may include different points of view about how to handle uncomfortable disputes in a family, between friends, with schoolmates, or with co-workers. A couple might struggle with whether and when to tell their daughter that she is adopted. Another couple might need to tell a child that the only father she has ever known is, in fact, her stepfather. Someone may be experiencing the need for support outside the family or friendship network. A woman might be facing surgery and need to tell her fear and distress to an understanding but emotionally uninvolved, person. As a responsible and caring person, her issues might include not wanting to burden her family. She may not realize that by leaving them out, she has not permitted the people she loves to show that they care about her.

Psychotherapy can be a place to air the individual concerns of each family member in a protected environment where there is some assurance that everyone will be heard. A young athlete may be struggling to cope with an injury as the short high school playing season passes by. A psychotherapist can be supportive in listening to her fears and in encouraging her efforts at rehabilitation. A psychotherapist might see a young boy who has moved into a new school and is having trouble making new friends. Together they could explore strategies for easing into a new neighborhood. In the meantime, the psychotherapist can be a support during the time it takes to find friends and become integrated into the new environment. A young girl might have been exposed to inappropriate sexual attention by an older relative—not coercion or molestation, but perhaps, a kiss or exposure. A psychotherapist can talk to her about guilt, embarrassment, and even mystery or pleasure. In therapy, sexual matters can be discussed and the relative responsibilities of adults and children clarified. In each of these situations, the discomfort is genuinely felt and people can be at the end of their own resources. Psychotherapy provides the time and the environment where life's concerns are explored, understood, and clearly resolved.

A burn may be more than an irritation; it may be a trauma. It disorders our lives because it is not expected. Its injury is deep and requires considerable time to heal. It may leave scars. These *problems* of life present us with greater complexity and perplexity. They are hard. The solutions are difficult to come to and may include leftover, unresolved problems of the past, a traumatic present, and/ or the anticipation of a devastating future. As endless as the experience may seem, as confusing as the emotions may be, problems have solutions. Sometimes the solutions are concrete, behavioral, or tangible. Sometimes the solutions involve the intangible domain of attitudes, values, and beliefs. Frequently, this ethereal sphere of life is where our problems are ultimately resolved.

A woman may come out of a marriage that in the long term proved to be unsatisfying. Because of the peculiar nature of our society, she may have never realized her own capacity and played only a supporting role in the unfolding potential of her husband. As he moved forward, she was left behind. This is not an infrequent story of the long years in professional preparation or the struggling years of building a business career. With the husband's success finally achieved, marriages sometimes dissolve and the husband acquires a much younger, prettier "trophy wife." Such wives are the equivalent of an award to honor the man's achievements and newfound status.

For the divorced first wife, the sudden and unwanted change in status may lead her to psychotherapy. This pattern reveals the deficiencies of our cultural expectations of women. The sacrifice of one person's development for the good of another may be seen as noble in the eyes of some, but in the counseling room it is exposed as a pathological state of affairs. Here the divorced woman may begin to explore her attitudes, values, and aspirations. She has to begin the process of finding her new place in the world.

Attitudinally, she may have to realize that if one person has loved her, another will find her lovable as well. She may need help to realilze that she has depended excessively on others to take care of her. Perhaps she must acknowledge that she has relied on her beauty or social skills to get by in life and has not developed her other potentials. Her new status may require her to enter or reenter the work force or go to college or to a graduate or professional school.

There is tragedy in such situations. It extends beyond the problems of interpersonal relationships. In the ongoing negotiations between men and women in our society, more than the men and more than the women must change. Society itself needs to be reshaped. The American Dream requires a new script. These are cultural concerns that must be addressed. In psychotherapy, we must proceed one person, one couple, one family at a time. In all this, there may be the substantial blossoming of a human being. More than once I have witnessed this transformation—from a woman who is dependent, wounded, and self-suppressing to one who is reasonably autonomous, coping, and self-respecting. Such women may still be challenged by life circumstances and social restraint, but they have moved from being victimized to using assertive coping skills that enable them to meet life on more equal terms.

I have also witnessed men who have come out of a marriage injured and unprepared for life outside its support. They have lost in equal measure their grasp on their life's dreams. I have seen some struggle with single parenthood after their wives have left. Their transformation can be wondrous. One widower, rough-cut and humble, was raising a daughter, and in psychotherapy, was able not only to mourn the loss of his wife but also to learn the skills of parenting. His efforts to cope with his situation all came together one night at a school activity. Again, our society often functions in mysterious ways. Blind to the diversity in families, the elementary school had organized a "mother and daughter night." So this man took his daughter to "mother and daughter" night. He sat with his daughter until it was time for the program to begin. One of the leaders of the event approached him and said, "It is time for the program to begin. Is Jenny's mother coming?" And he said, "I am Jenny's mother."

Wouldn't it have been wonderful to have been present at that moment—the silence broken only by the sound of a false cultural presumption cracking? I had the joy of hearing this relatively unsophisticated man report the incident; he said, "You know, right then it became clear to me that whether Jenny's mother is here or not, I am the only parent she has." In psychotherapy, the struggle to redefine his role as a father had been exploded. The issue wasn't what a mother should do or what a father should do; it was about raising a child.

In another story about change, a woman in her thirties ended a marriage. She had married at about age twenty and was now working and raising her two children. She entered psychotherapy for a number of reasons. A part of her adjustment from marriage to being single involved dating. In many respects, even though she had been married and given birth to two children, she was socially and sexually naive. She alluded frequently to the expectation of the men she was dating that the two would be sexually intimate in a relatively short time—if not on the first date, then certainly by the third. She was shocked that sex was openly discussed and offered.

Whereas she was embarrassed, her dates seemed confused at her reaction. In one meeting, she said, "I think my problem is that I am living in the 1990s with a value system from the 1950s." Later, she also experienced a shift in conceptualization. She said, "Sex isn't the issue any more. I am thirty-six years old and I am acting like I am seventeen. But that isn't it, either. It isn't that sex is wrong or bad and I have to be seduced to give it up. That's thinking like a seventeen-year-old. It's that I haven't been willing to act like an adult. I haven't been willing to take responsibility for my own sexual needs. I am the one who decides. If I want to agree to sex, then that's me deciding. If I don't, then it is because I don't want to. It isn't having to be convinced or seduced. I think I am learning to be an adult." She was involved in the process of moving from an introjected value system to a more internalized one. In less lofty terms, she was finding her own way to be in the world.

Not all problems involve interpersonal relationships. A person might be depressed, and the source of the depression might be vague and slippery. Anxiety is by definition fear without a clearly defined object. In these situations, psychotherapy is a time of exploring, searching, and clarifying. The issue at this point in therapy is not solutions but clarity and understanding. It is also a time of support and reassurance that some resolution can be realized.

Some burns can be more than traumatic; they can be life threatening. These *dilemmas* of life defy solutions. Some involve mutual exclusivity. If I marry Jennifer, I cannot marry Juanita. Life can present us with situations in which one option is as equally unfortunate as the next. Turn to the left and we are faced with turmoil; turn to the right and we are confronted with chaos. The Existential thinkers have written eloquently of human despair. Jean Paul Sartre's play *No Exit* presents us with characters caught in the human dilemma.[1] We are trapped in Hell and there is no way out. It is that way for some of us. The situations and events facing us have no satisfying end. An unwanted pregnancy is a human dilemma. This seems tragically and unmercifully so for adolescents. Pregnancy for a sixteen- or seventeen-year-old, in our society, darkens the future. The possibilities for an advanced education, a decent job, a stable marriage, and a wholesome life for the child are all tenuous if the mother tries to raise the baby. If she gives the baby up for adoption, she may be faced with deep, unremitting lifelong feelings of sorrow and loss. The child may grow into adulthood puzzled, confused, and wondering about the circumstances that led to his or her adoption. If the teenager decides for an abortion, she may face guilt and despair. She may be left with relentless longing for what might have been. She may find little sympathy in our fractionated, opinionated, and polarized society. None of these options is gratifying. Each exacts an emotional price. Life continues for people who face insoluble dilemmas, but they are marked by the experience.

What solution is there for the death of a child? What explanation satisfies a parent whose baby dies at birth? Death at the end of life can be understood. Death at the beginning of life robs the future and destroys dreams, and the memory will not go away. When children die, our sense of innocence and control in the world dies with them. Hardened soldiers, police officers, physicians, nurses, and paramedics may see death frequently and treat it as a matter of fact; yet find themselves touched and unprepared for the death of a child. Each of us is unprepared. Sensibility is torn from us. There is no center. There is no resolution. Parents of children who have died by whatever means may grieve differently, but they grieve forever. The death of a child is unnatural and it has no resolution. What, then, is the purpose of psychotherapy in the face of human dilemmas that have no solution? It is this. No matter how deep the wound, if we survive, we can heal. Healing may not leave us unscarred, but it permits us to continue our lives. Continued life carries with it hope. Psychotherapy is a statement of hope. It can guarantee us nothing, yet it promises us that in the depths of our misery there is the possibility that if we can endure, we may prevail. If we can endure, we may yet in the undetermined future, find meaning. For some, there is no future in a determination of terminal disease or impending death from any cause. What role can a psychotherapist play here? It may be only to sit quietly with a dying person. It may be to talk about death openly, to hear the fear, the hope, the despair, the loneliness, the sense of incompleteness. It may be to take the time to explore mutually what peace there may be in death. There may be time to review a rich and fulfilling life. There may be time to review lingering sorrow. The therapist's role may be to let the family express their fears, or to act as a buffer between the factions of a family as one of its members dies. There may be no role that is satisfactory for the helper. This is a dilemma that psychotherapists must face. It has no solution. We cannot be of help to all of the people all the time. We do what we can when we can; we must make our peace with this.

117

19

Your Past Is Not Your Potential

*Y*our past is a fact; it is not a binding judgment. Perhaps one of the least helpful and most depressing concepts in psychological theory is the one claiming that our life's path is determined by our experiences in early childhood. We have all heard that as the twig inclines, so grows the tree. Some would have us believe that our lives are determined in our infancy by the toss of capricious dice; our path is set for good or ill, our future happiness is determined by unthinking fate in the accidental assignment of this set of parents or that set of environmental conditions. Even more deterministic is the idea that our lives and psychological development are set with little variability through genes donated by our parents. Of course, if chance gives us good genes, good parents, and a good environment, the sky's the limit. However, if we get shortchanged on genetics, have lousy parents, and live in a crummy neighborhood, then kiss a decent life good-bye because the path is set.

In truth, life can seem to collude with catastrophic adversity to ruin the most promising potential. Good lives are ended and promise is never realized for too many. We are wrong, however, if we conclude from these tragic circumstances that those who somehow manage to survive their lousy childhoods have persevered in vain. It is fundamentally wrong to decide that the die has been cast and that they have survived only to be condemned by early experience. Short of death and physical damage to the brain, those who live through a dreadful childhood do have a chance, and for anyone to claim that their potential is forever denied and cannot be fulfilled is malicious. This is the danger of a philosophy that teaches that the past determines the present. However powerful early life experiences are, the capacity of human beings to transcend them is overwhelmingly evident in every profession—from marketing to medicine, from trucking to teaching, from letters to law.

In my own experience, I number among my university professors a Hispanic, former gang member from East Los Angeles; two high school dropouts; and one person diagnosed as mentally retarded as a youth. Whatever reasons we might now give for their achievements, we see clearly that those who closed the book on their potential as children closed it prematurely. In my own experience, I have witnessed the gathering strength of ravaged youth collect itself, rise to its full height, and step into the future with renewed hope and promise. Do not tell such people that their past has determined their future; do not tell them that after survival there cannot be satisfaction, success, and achievement. Philosophy must be revised when confronted with actual life.

We cannot deny that people with devastating early life experiences must struggle to overcome their hardships or that chance may give a leg up to some and shrink the odds for others. I have seen, however, that human beings are made of remarkable stuff. Battered, abused, mistreated, rejected, neglected, abandoned, molested, they have survived every dire condition imaginable and yet many have endured, survived, and overcome these hardships to live good and decent lives. This knowledge should in no way allow us to reduce our efforts to create a world where decent living conditions should be the birthright of every person. I don't advocate any lack of concern or lack of compassion for people whose lives are diminished by circumstance. I am arguing that any philosophy that sells short the human capacity to overcome tragedy is specious—false, erroneous, faulty, mistaken, and, in a word, wrong.

Certainly, our lives may be influenced by past events, but are our lives *determined* by past events? There is much difference between a belief that early life experiences unalterably set the course for all future events. Surely previous events impact us in some way. To believe that we are determined by the past speaks of rigid limitations and pessimism. There is little hope in such a belief. My experience as a psychotherapist teaches me that the past is not as condemning as some have assumed. People do survive and some even transcend their perilous beginnings to thrive. There is hope in the world.

Do not think, however, that hope implies a guarantee of a successful outcome. Optimism is a point of view that teaches that we can reasonably expect the best possible outcome. It holds that the world, as it is, is the best possible world. On the other hand, pessimism is a belief that adversity is inevitable and that we should expect the worst. Neither of these extremes deserves much support in the real world. Hope is neither of these. Hope is a belief that the future is unknown. The word is not written. The page has not turned. The book is not closed. Hope is the belief that somewhere in the passage of time, in the turn of fortune, in the struggle to survive, the pen will come to us and whatever is inscribed will be written by our own hand.

Some experiences are forever. Write and the word is written. Turn the page. Others are not. For some, even the most crushing ordeal can fade and, in time and struggle, come to be viewed merely as a fact of their lives, its force diluted by survival and assertive hope. Coupled with possibility, hope gives lie to any belief that misfortune ends any chance of happiness. Whether we are formed by experience, imitate those who raise us, or through some other press of circumstance, I have been taught by clients in psychotherapy that we can create new experiences, unlearn old behaviors, alter our attitudes, and forge new lives from old.

I have learned from clients in psychotherapy important lessons. What doesn't kill us, we can endure. What we can endure, we can survive. What we can survive, we can overcome. What we can overcome, we can transform. These are the lessons of psychotherapy.

The past does not determine the present. Bent twigs may straighten themselves, given the possibility. A walk in the forest will often show us a tree that was smothered by underbrush and shadowed by larger trees, which has grown sideways and twisted until it too found the light and warmth of the sun—and from that time, it has grown straight and tall. Many have reported a similar history. Raised in the shadow of cruelty, their lives stunted and crooked, they survived and found light and warmth. Our past is not our potential. Our potential is found in hope. Hope underlies psychotherapy.

According to modern psychological thought, we are as likely to be pulled by the future as we are to be pushed by the past. If we want to understand a person, knowing her hopes, dreams, and aspirations may be more important than knowing her history. When I meet people who have come from cruel circumstances and have survived, even prospered, I know that somewhere in those lives a window to the future appeared. They saw the possibility, climbed through it, and walked into a life different from what circumstances predicted. How could we be here at all if tragedy and despair set the limits on human accomplishment? A person's hopes and dreams have more predictive power than the past. To view any human act in terms of what a person was trying to get is certainly as explanatory as viewing it in terms of what he or she was trying to get away from. Anxiety may stem as much from being cut off from our goals as it does from avoiding objects of fear. Depression can be the sadness of failed dreams as often as a response to psychological injury. Anger may be a response to being blocked from what we want as well as a defensive reaction against some past hurt.

Much that is evil and much that is good stems from the pursuit of what human beings hope to accomplish. Our past is not our potential; our hopes are. Even in despair, we may hope for a better life. Hope permits us to seize the possibility that presents itself. Even more important, hope can be active, creating possibilities. As we seek to understand human beings, it is more important to know that we are reaching for the stars than that we came from the sea.

20

Choices Versus Decisions

We don't choose to be hurt. We do not choose to be depressed, injured, burdened, or disheartened. Yet a person might come into psychotherapy and say, "I don't know why I am unhappy. I am the one who chose the divorce. Now I am so sad and guilty. I know I don't have a right to feel that way because I chose to end the marriage."

Feeling guilty over a choice may not make much sense, but in the situation above, *no choice has been made*. How is this possible?

This is not a chapter on words and their meanings, but words are the devices we use to convey meanings and concepts. Therefore, we need to spend some time discussing them. We have been enveloped by words since birth. Words are the tools of thought, and thought is the source of meaning. Since birth, perhaps before, we have been learning the power of words. Words can be the source of our liberty or of our psychological imprisonment.

I have shown this chapter to a number of professional readers and they all ask similar questions: Why spend an entire chapter on words? Why not just call the situation you describe a forced choice versus a free choice? They have suggested that I am making too much of a small thing. Perhaps, they are right. Still, my experience with people who are struggling with situations has convinced me that the difference is important. Therefore, I am going to risk this chapter on words with you and the meanings of these words in psychotherapy.

What of the word *choice?* More than a dictionary definition is involved here. I write of its psychological meaning. Even so, I invite you to consider the dictionary definition of *choice. Choice* does mean selection, but it is a selection of a particular sort. *Choice* implies the right to select *freely* from desirable options. I believe this particular definition has important psychological meaning for us. This definition suggests that we do not choose to be hurt, injured, or damaged emotionally or psychologically in our relationships.

So what is wrong with the earlier statement from the person who described sadness and guilt over leaving a marriage? First, we feel the way we feel, and rights have little to do with it; and, while sadness is perfectly appropriate, guilt is unnecessary. Second, few of us choose to end a marriage. Wait a minute, you might protest, if people don't choose to end a marriage, why are so many marriages ending? Clearly, many Americans are unhappy in their present marriages and seek to get out of them, but it is wholly false to conclude from these frightful statistics that we have chosen to end a relationship with someone we love, or once loved. On the other hand, most of us did choose to get married in the first place. Few of us probably feel guilty shortly after the wedding ceremony. Some of us did not choose to marry and that is just the point. Some of us entered marriage under duress of one sort or another. Most of us leave marriage under duress. In these last two cases, no choice has been made—*decisions* have been made.

A choice is a peculiarly human act. It is a selection made freely and after consideration. I am not certain how often we have choices presented to us. We may not even remember them because they have so little impact on us. Choices are natural, easy, and free. We choose between something that is desirable and something that is unappealing. It is not emotionally draining to select between something we want and something we don't. That is what a choice is, and we are unlikely to experience guilt after the selection. Entering marriage is like that. Leaving marriage isn't.

When we enter marriage, we are choosing to be close, to be intimate, to have a partner, to have our emotional needs met, and not be alone. We are creating the opportunity to share lives and experiences, and to be able to tell somebody our joys and split our sorrows. Marriage is an affirmation that we are ultimately lovable and worthy of commitment. It is a choice because we are giving up something for marriage: living alone, eating alone, having nobody with whom to share the daily ins and outs, and so forth. I am not speaking here about sharing an apartment, but of sharing a life— emotionally, psychologically, spiritually, financially. Marriage means a joint bank account, insurance premiums, and in-laws. My point is that people who think marriage is a burden do not *choose* to marry. They may marry, but they don't choose it. People choose marriage when they see it as desirable and being single as not. That is a choice.

Let's examine four possible situations. These four may include all the possible combinations of human situations: (1) Win-Lose; (2) Win-Win; (3) Win/Lose-Win/Lose; and (4) Lose-Lose. The first two involve choices. The last two do not. There is little if any stress involved in the first two. The first is companionship versus loneliness. It is "chocolate ice cream with a cherry on top" versus "eat your spinach." The second involves winning the lottery and choosing between yearly or monthly payments. Your selection really doesn't make any difference; you and other people will be equally happy. That is a *choice,* freely arrived at and satisfying. This isn't hard.

Being faced with a situation in which picking one alternative rules out another, however, is stressful. This is not a *choice;* it is a *decision.* The word *decide* means merely that you end a vacillation, a doubt, a dispute by making up your mind. It means only that you settle on a course of action. It does not mean that the course of action is satisfying or freely selected. It means only an end to a particular situation. This is a dilemma. The most talented musician in high school may be faced with scholarships in music and premedical studies. If she selects one, she loses the other. She cannot pursue a career in music and become a physician. What should she do? A young man is offered a promotion in the company, but it means the family has to move to Arizona. His wife would have to give up her job and she doesn't want to move away from her family. If he stays where he is, it is unlikely he will advance in the company. If he goes now he could be promoted, but he will sacrifice his family life. If he stays his family will be happy, but his career will suffer. What should he do?

Equally difficult and even more frightening is living in an abusive marriage or leaving that marriage to face single parenthood without a job or financial resources. There is no choice in this situation. It is what is commonly called a no win situation. Nevertheless, the present situation is intolerable. On one side lies physical danger and on the other isolation, loneliness, continued fear, and possible poverty. Where is the choice here?

An adolescent discovers she is pregnant. She is seventeen years old. Her options include abortion, adoption, and single parenthood. The very pregnancy itself may not have come about through choice. She may have been forced into sex or pressured into it out of fear of losing her boyfriend. These are not choices. They are decisions that have to be made. They may be forced on us or be the result of other bad decisions. Whatever the case, the dilemma has to be resolved. The person has to decide what to do. A *decision* merely brings a dilemma to an end. It answers a question. It concludes a situation. It may momentarily reduce stress; it may not. A young woman decides on abortion. A young man opts to pursue his career. What follows may be relief, guilt, anger, depression, or other emotional reactions. The stress and duress may be diminished, but new complications may arise because of the decision. Decisions follow decisions. Frequently, time determines the quality of a decision. Its value is impacted by subsequent events. Its outcome for good or ill is influenced by resolve, purpose, circumstance, and even chance.

I would not spend our time on these words if I did not consider them important. The importance, of course, is not in the definitions but in the psychological consequences of the actions they imply. The consequence lies not in the definitions but in our understanding of the human dilemmas they represent.

There appear to be at least five differences between situations that invite choice and those that require decisions. First, choices do not lead to psychotherapy. People do not seek out psychotherapists to tell us good news. Psychotherapy is a process of exploring, understanding, and finding coping skills for problems. Decisions, for reasons we discuss below, may lead a person to psychotherapy seeking help in coping with the emotions that result from decision making. Decisions may create guilt, depression, shame, and uncertainty—all good reasons for entering psychotherapy.

Second, choices are unforced, freely made. The consideration that is given to a choice is unfettered by contaminating influences. The options are clear, and although they need some consideration, choice situations do not require precise, calculated, or labored thinking for a satisfying resolution. Decisions are compelled and made under duress. The stress comes because the decision will demand a loss, no matter what is decided. An irony is that decisions require clear, precise thinking, yet stress and threat create muddy thinking. Sometimes we must decide matters in a crisis and have too little information to make a sound decision. Sometimes we agonize in a flood of information. Whatever the circumstances, the decision is not made freely.

Third, choices are made quickly, spontaneously, often immediately. The issues are clear, the outcome is inviting. There is no need to ponder long. I have been drafted by the Colorado Rockies professional baseball team and I have to choose between them and Buck's Tavern slowpitch softball team. Humm, what should I do? After careful consideration, I think I'll try professional baseball. Right! The choice is decisive.

Decisions may be impulsive or delayed. The issues are clouded, the outcome is discouraging. Look at the difference. I am a bright young woman who has been offered a scholarship to the state university. I live in a family that does not value higher education and expects me to continue working as a waitress in the family restaurant, get married, and live two blocks from home. What should I do? Should I seize the opportunity and offend my family or honor my family and close the door on possibility. I might, in a fury of emotion, lash out at my family and tell them that they are rigid and old-fashioned and they can't stop me from being better than they are. I might, on the other hand, in a moment of obligation and guilt, tell them that I am staying home and following family tradition. Either decision, made in a frenzy of emotion, can be impetuous and reckless. To escape the emotion, the young woman may delay the decision, hoping that something will happen to make it unnecessary. Often, a decision is put off with the hope that some-one or something will make it. Regardless, there is a sense of dis-tress and it stems from the losses any decision will incur.

Fourth, choices are mostly satisfying. After a person makes a choice, freely considered, the outcome is pleasing and gratifying. The person is happy. He or she has a sense of closure. Decisions often have an opposite quality. Even after a stressful decision is made, people second guess themselves. They worry. The solution they have selected is often unsatisfying and nagging. We make de-cisions, then think "What if..."and "If only..." Again, decisions re-quire losses. After a decision, we may be momentarily relieved, but soon we become aware of the losses and indecisiveness sets in. This is a time when people reverse themselves. Now they decide the other alternative was better. So they apologize, seek forgiveness, make amends, and go in the opposite direction. Again, they may feel re-lief, but nagging reminders will surface about why they made the first decision. They may begin flip-flopping as pressure from one source or another leads to change after change in the decision. Others may stick to their original decision, suffering through their discontent and hanging on in the hope that their distress will, like early morning fog, drift away in time. This is often the point at which people enter psychotherapy. They have made a decision and it has not ended their stress. It may have ended the situation, but now they are faced with unexpected emotions. Guilt, depression, anxiety, anger, and helplessness may all come after a decision, and people find themselves out of options. Choices satisfy; deci-sions nag.

Fifth, choices bring closure. They open possibilities and lead to the future. Freely made and satisfying, a choice permits a person to move on, go on unburdened by second guessing. A decision, on the other hand, often brings uncertainty and lack of resolution. A di-vorce may end a marriage; it doesn't end a relationship. The deci-sion may end an intolerable situation, but it leaves disruption in its wake. These waves of vexation and regret wash through life and leave a troubled sea. Decisions force us to focus constantly on the past, carrying its burdens into the future. Laden with the unhappi-ness of a forced decision, life feels heavy and irksome.

These difference are felt most keenly when a person is trapped in a cycle of doubt. All decisions carry losses. Greater losses cary more dissatisfaction. Life presents us with both choices and decisions. I am not certain what stimulus for growth choices provide. It may well be that the decisions in our lives are our best teachers. As we grapple with decisions, we may strengthen ourselves emotionally. In dealing with losses, we may empower ourselves psychologically and validate ourselves as worthwhile persons. Make no mistake, however, it is making the decision and seeing the successful outcome, not enduring the troubling life situation itself, which strengthen and empower us.

21

On Perfection

*J*n his poem "Disiderata," Max Ehrmann offers this advice:
Beyond a wholesome discipline, be gentle with yourself.[1] Ah,
were it so for us. A wholesome discipline that permitted striving
and achievement. A wholesome discipline that permitted balance
in our lives among the demands of society, career, family, and self.
It seems out of reach for many in our society. Among the most
troubled souls who come to psychotherapy are those whose psychological structures include a perfectionistic component. Whatever
efforts they make are always unsatisfactory. No amount of time is
sufficient. No effort is adequate. No idea is sound. Every attempt is
crude and flawed. No project is ever good enough. Every presenta-
tion is critiqued and found wanting. Perfection is a cruel and relentless master.

Perfection means to be flawless, without defect, but when this
definition of flawlessness is applied to human beings and human
relationships, it corrupts the human spirit. That definition fosters
emotional damage. Each of us knows the lonely acquaintance who
can't seem to find the right companion. The search for Mr. or Ms.
Right begins each time with hope and ends with rejection. There is
always a flaw of behavior, character, or morality that suggest the
search must continue. These people aren't looking for a good man
or a solid woman; they are searching for an image of perfection.

We may know people who were fine through courtship, engagement, and a year or so of marriage. Now they are unhappy. They
might say their partners don't seem committed to marriage the

way they are and they can offer a list of flaws or shortcomings compared to the way marriage should be. Many of us, perhaps all, carry into our unions an image of what marriage will be like. Most of us realize that these images are naive or misguided, and we adapt them to conform with reality. For some, the perfectionistic image is so unyielding that the partner must adapt or leave. The image survives at the expense of the partner.

A more bitter pattern is one in which the perfectionistic ideal is centered on children. Imagine a perfect couple planning the ideal pregnancy. They select the most sought after obstetrician and the immaculate hospital with a birthing room decorated just as they imagined it would be. They consult family, friends, and baby magazines for the design of the nursery. The wallpaper, decorations, crib, and stimulating baby toys are chosen with extreme care. The delivery is perfect. Only then do the parents discover that the wrong baby was born. This isn't the baby they expected at all. First, it's a boy. He cries. He spits up. He doesn't sleep through the night. He makes unreasonable demands at all hours of the day and night. His hygiene is appalling. They wanted a baby like the one in the magazines or the movies.

In each of these scenes, the problem lies with the meaning of perfection and the inflexibility that stems from its definition. Where can such cruel expectations come from? There seem to be at least two possible explanations for the problems perfection can cause in the lives of people.

First, they fail to understand that perfection itself is an ideal. An ideal, by definition, exists in the mind. It is a mental image, an abstraction. Some people fail to bridge the difference between the "image" and the "real." They reify the image. To reify means to regard an abstraction as something concrete or material, to believe that a mental image exists as real. Some people, for whatever confusing reasons, actually do believe there is such a thing as a perfect partner, a perfect marriage, or a perfect baby. Believing this, their lives are characterized by disappointment. The most crushing beliefs do not center in others; they lie within. Some people think that they themselves should be perfect. Constantly in touch with their own flaws, they live in a state of perpetual self-condemnation for their shortcomings. In such people, there is no peace.

Second, some people believe that perfection is rare. They think that there are magic moments in life when expectation meets reality. They don't happen often; but when they do, it is a miracle. Some special confluence of expectation, performance, and completion occurs, and the result is flawless, without parallel. People with these beliefs live for that moment; for the rest of life, they wait. They might revere the arts and search for the painting or sculpture, musical performance or dance, drama, poem, or novel that conforms to their ideal. In all this, they might never realize that perfection lies in their own mind and not in the object.

These problems begin when they transform a mental image into a material reality. The resolution lies in confronting or dematerializing the false belief—that life exists without flaws, or that human relationships must be constantly fulfilling, or that those we love must live up to our expectations and when they don't they are undeserving of our love. Resolution cannot come if we believe that we cannot live together in harmony and love if we fall short of an ideal. There can be no resolution as long as we hold the unyielding and demanding conception that the ideal and the corporeal must be the same.

In life, perfection is what happens when no better outcome is possible. One of the rarest accomplishments in all of sports is the perfect game in baseball. A perfect game is accomplished when a pitcher completes a game with no hits, no runs, no walks, no errors; and no opposing runners reaching base. It is a wonderful moment in baseball. But what does it mean? Does it mean that the pitcher did not make a single mistake? Does it mean that each pitch was perfect? Does it mean that each pitch was a strike and that not a single ball was called by the umpire? Of course not. It doesn't mean any of those things.

Here is another example. The score is tied in the bottom of the last inning. There is a runner on third base and there are two outs. The batter swings at the pitch and hits it. It is a little blooper fly ball just between the shortstop and the left fielder that drops in for a single. The runner scores and the game is won. The announcer might say, "Well, it wasn't pretty but that single scores the winning run." Here is my point. The problem is not with the batter or the blooper; it is with the announcer. He or she did not recognize a moment of perfection when it happened. The *image* of perfection is one of pristine beauty. The *image* is so powerful that when perfection occurs, we do not always recognize it. There can be no better outcome for the batting team than for the batter to hit the ball in such a way that the winning run scores. (Perfection for the defensive team is, of course, an entirely different matter.) That is perfection in practical terms. Life is messy. Babies cry, wake up at inconvenient times, and pee in their pants. Human beings have the capacity both to fulfill one another's needs and expectations and to frustrate them. As far as human relationships are concerned, our best outcomes may be accomplished and still be flawed. The best outcomes we can expect or desire come frequently. In human relationships, we can learn to call them perfection; they are the best outcomes we can hope for, and they come with warts or they are common in many ways. What is destructive is our inability to appreciate the common, everyday perfection of life. This unforgiving conception of the ideal invites people to punish themselves as they continually reject life while trying to attain a state of impossible purity.

Psychotherapy is a time and a process that lets us explore and clarify what we genuinely want and what is ultimately acceptable to us in attaining our goals. It provides a climate in which punishing beliefs and their origins may be exposed. Whatever their origins, they exist as mental images, as unobtainable ideals.

There is a science fiction story in which an alien satellite is brought on board a spaceship. As the story unfolds, we learn that this particular satellite was created from the collision of two separate satellites from two separate worlds. In the scrambled self-repair, the mission of one satellite to search out new life and the mission of the other to destroy a dangerous biological infestation on its home planet had been merged and perverted into a mission of searching out and destroying imperfect biological life. Naturally, the crew of the spaceship, being human, were in immediate danger from a mission to destroy imperfection!

In the science fiction world, it is no stretch to imagine that a satellite might go awry and end up endangering humanity. I am not sure there is any great meaning in this episode other than demonstrating that science fiction writers are a creative bunch, but I see a parallel between that wandering satellite and perfectionistic thinking. The perfectionistic component of a person's psychological structure, a satellite of the self, through uncompromising judgment, drives the person to unreasonable striving. In its rigid assessment, the perfectionistic component fails to note that the best possible outcome has occurred and been rejected as flawed. This is, logically, an imperfect judgment and one in which the perfectionistic part is itself flawed. It certainly follows that if solutions judged as flawed by the perfectionistic part should be rejected, then a flawed perfectionistic part should be rejected as well. In the resulting confusion of such a self-examination, we should not pass up the opportunity to help the person build a more realistic, more gentle, and more wholesome psychological structure, one in which striving is disciplined and judgments are more reasonable.

22

⌇

Die Gedanken Sind Frei
(The Thoughts Are Free)

*T*here is no such thing as a bad emotion, yet many in our society are tormented by their thoughts and feelings about their thoughts and feelings. The old saw says, "I'm sick and tired of being sick and tired." Many feel guilty over the decisions they have made in their lives and then become angry with themselves because they feel guilty. Some might feel anger at a perceived slight or tangible wrong and experience guilt over their emotional reaction followed by perplexity about why they are guilty. This layering of thoughts and feelings may drive us further and further away from original experience and reasoning. Such persons could profit from the words of a song sung by American prisoners of war in Germany during World War II. *Die Gedanken sind frei* means literally, "the thoughts are free." The prisoners were telling their captors that only their bodies were imprisoned, their minds were free. If there were a version dedicated to the emotions, it might read *Die Gefühle sind frei*—"the feelings are free." We feel what we feel and we do not need to punish ourselves for feelings alone.

One function of psychotherapy is to help clients uncover or clarify their feelings. This process contributes to another of the myths of psychotherapy. So many believe that psychotherapy is a practice of examining the past. There is a difference, however, between analyzing past events and exploring the wrappings of apparent thoughts and feelings to come to a more central, accurate, and primary understanding of the causes of our behavior. In one analogy, this process is like peeling an onion. Yet the analogy has its limitation. When we have peeled away all the layers, nothing is left. Sometimes that is an unsatisfying result, but other times it is desirable. What clients feared is revealed as nonexistent. The heart of the issue is exposed as mist—as fear without substance.

Another analogy relies more on images of oranges, apples, or peaches in which the exploration uncovers a core or a seed. These tangible causes are hidden in the pulp, surrounded by layers of protection both hardened and tender. These are the defenses created to shield unpleasant thoughts, feelings, behaviors, or events that began a process of ineffective living. Finding a prime cause for them is worthwhile. It is also rare. One of the myths of Hollywood, television, and dramatized fiction is that human behavior can be traced to a single cause. This notion may make good entertainment, but it has little to do with our lives. We do not have to delve deeply into the human condition to discover that the sources of human behavior are multi-causal, multi-influenced, or multi-determined.

We are left, then, with the concept that some of psychotherapy is dedicated to exploring with people what their expectations of psychotherapy are and what assumptions they have brought with them to the process. Exploration is exactly what they are going to do with themselves in psychotherapy. The task for individuals is to explore what their expectations are of themselves, what assumptions about themselves they have brought with them, and why such expectations and assumptions might trouble them.

This process of exploration can be furthered when clients understand that there is no need to judge their feelings as positive or negative. Exploration opens up with the recognition that there is no such thing as an improper feeling. Initially, this is most important for the psychotherapist. Recognizing and accepting that people feel what they feel permits a nonjudgmental attitude and genuine understanding. Later, as people come to accept their feelings, they too can move to genuine understanding of their behavior and motivations.

Beliefs play a key role in our lives. The belief that some emotions are positive and some negative can itself become a block to understanding our motivations. If we consider anger to be an inappropriate emotion, we might experience guilt when we get angry. Guilt may be followed by confusion over the reasons for the guilt. The outcome of this confusion is that we are alienated from our original experience by three layers of feelings. We might then spend time trying to figure out our confusion and be led even further afield. This circular process begins in the belief that a particular emotion should not be felt. Much clutter is swept aside by adopting the attitude that thoughts and feelings are free. When clients can view their thoughts without condemning them, at least one obstacle to effective living has been removed. There is other work to be done, but guilt over thoughts can be eliminated.

Our emotions are not ends; they are clues. They are signals that an attitude, conviction, or belief is being affirmed or challenged. Let me give you a personal example. Years ago, I would be embarrassed when in the midst of seemingly ordinary conversations my voice would crack and my eyes would tear up. I simply saw myself as highly emotional and needing to control myself. Through time, I gained a different understanding. My cracking voice and teary eyes came to mean that hidden somewhere in that ordinary conversation was something of importance to me. I had touched on something tender, valuable, significant, and meaningful. I came to value these moments. Rather than being embarrassed, I was prompted to explore the sensitive meaning. Now, in those moments when my voice wavers, I have become comfortable acknowledging to others that something they said has touched me, and I need to think about it. Freed from embarrassment, I am better able to understand my behavior.

Our emotions are not the cause of difficulty in our relationships. It is what we do in response to our emotions that often creates problems. If we feel jealous, we don't have to condemn ourselves. If we beat up our partner in response to our jealousy, *that* is a significant problem. If the role of the emotions is to provide clues to inner meanings, how should we act on them? Should our actions be different for negative and positive emotions? There is, as you might expect, divided opinion on these questions.

In America, we have fluctuated between controling and expressing emotions and have held different standards of expression and control for males and females. A traditional idea has been that men should control their emotions and that women are permitted to be more expressive of the positive emotions. It might be "unladylike" to express a negative emotion such as anger. A man might be given more latitude in expressing negative emotions, but would be considered "ungentlemanly" if he lost control, an act that would be taken as a sign of weakness. These traditional ideas regarding controlling and expressing anger have been challenged by those who saw such controlled emotions as psychologically damaging, and in the area of gender politics, considered the double standard for males and females to be unacceptable.

In the 1960s and 1970s, we experienced something of a cultural upheaval if not a revolution. Authenticity was celebrated, and this meant being truthful about our feelings and the clear expression of those feelings to one another. The need was to "get those feelings out." People were taught to express their feelings directly. If someone was an object of anger, that person should be told immediately and directly. If we could not express our anger toward someone directly, we were taught to "get that anger out" by banging on pillows or whacking away with rubber bats. The first idea was weak on expression and the second was weak on control.

As values evolved, especially in psychotherapy, we learned that holding emotions in was unproductive and expressing emotions freely was ineffective. Part of the resolution came in understanding the effect of the emotion being expressed. Tender emotions, for example, when expressed directly and clearly, have positive and constructive effects. Appreciation, gratitude, or affection nearly always produce a favorable reaction. Anger, sarcasm, ridicule, or criticism typically evoke antagonistic responses. Thus, expressing tender emotions seems to aid relationships and expressing negative emotions seems to hinder and harm them. Still, it was clear that holding in negative emotions was generally not good. Many people seem able to hold them for only so long, at which point they explode in violence. All the suppressed negative feelings would come flooding out when some seemingly small incident has broken the dam.

As we use our emotions to help us understand ourselves, we find that the negative emotions (anger, jealously, envy) are ineffective in improving human relationships if they are expressed as they are experienced. If I am angry at a business partner, I do little to resolve the situation if I call the man an idiot and smack him with a calculator. A more helpful approach is to talk about our feelings of anger, rather than expressing them directly: "I was angry about the overdrawn account and need to do something about it." In human relationships, this approach neither suppresses the emotion nor attacks another person. Problem solving and discussion have the greatest chance of success when negative emotions are expressed descriptively and nonviolently, and when positive emotions are expressed personally.

23

Living with Purpose

I want to take a chance on life before chance takes my life. As simplistic, and perhaps as maudlin, as this sentiment seems, it lies at the heart of healthy psychological living. I am hard pressed to think of any human endeavor that does not involve risks. Relationships risk rejection. Writing risks criticism. Financial investments risk loss. Psychotherapy itself involves risks. It may fail, leaving the person stuck in his or her life predicament. It may work, involving the person in exploring personally meaningful and painful life change.

There is clearly a paradox involved in this business of risks. Some of us seek vainly to insulate ourselves to avoid painful anxiety. Insulation is one way to try to avoid risks. Some of us try to reduce anxiety by becoming dependent on others to shield us from distressing situations—as if by seeking the shelter of childhood, life will be less frightening. Some lash out to drive others away. Aggressively controlling their contacts, they hope to reduce their internal anxiety. People who are depressed experience a loss of both physical and psychological energy and withdraw from human commerce. Here is the paradox. The anxious seek to control risks and, in their efforts, risk alienating people. The depressed, because of real or imagined injuries, withdraw from human interaction—the source of and the relief from their depression.

We are faced with a decision. We can live our lives on purpose and risk failure. Of course, we risk success as well. We can renounce purpose and risk the dangers of happenstance. Look at this scene.

I would like to have a pocket watch for Christmas. I hope to get one. I write a letter to Santa. I wish upon a star. In fact, I do pretty much everything *except* tell my family that the gift I would most like to have is a pocket watch. What are the odds that of all the possible gifts available, my family will guess I want a pocket watch?

In this peculiar situation, acting without purpose is a strategy for disappointment. It leads to an often-played script in which one partner is disappointed and angry because he or she feels slighted. One might say, "You don't love me!" The other replies, "Of course, I love you." "No you don't. If you loved me you would have given me flowers on my birthday like you did last year." "I didn't know you wanted flowers." "Well, you should have!" This is a scene in which one partner forces the other into the role of mind reader. Because wishes are not stated, the partner is forced to guess. It is a cruel and destructive game. Conversely, I might say, "I would love a pocket watch for Christmas." Other things being equal, what are the odds now? There's no guarantee, but the balance has certainly shifted in my favor. When I state my wishes, desires, and needs clearly and realistically, I give a gift to others. They know their efforts are going to be appreciated.

Of course, living with purpose is not concerned mainly with such trivial matters as gifts at Christmas. It is concerned not only with the peripheral, but with the core aspects of life. Purpose is more central to the core of life than it is to the peripheral. I can plop a dollar down on a "quick pick" in the lottery rather than carefully selecting my numbers because I'm not risking much and the odds are the same anyway. Selecting a partner for marriage is an entirely different proposition. We don't call up the agency and say, "I'm ready to get married. Send over anybody." More realistically, in human relationships, one person may hope fervently that things work out. He or she may leave things to chance and pray for the best. Out of fear of what will happen by facing an issue openly, a person may risk losing a personal relationship through neglect.

I am not fond of mechanical metaphors to help explain human behavior, but one seems appropriate here. Ignore any piece of machinery and it will break down eventually. Bicycle chains need oil. Automobile wheels need alignment. Coffee makers need cleaning.

To avoid maintenance is to invite sour coffee. It is true for human relationships as well. It is true of ourselves. Our relationships need care. We need to maintain ourselves. Shit does happen. Good doesn't just happen; it is planned and maintained. When shit happens, we can clean it up.

Living with purpose is a process of self-knowledge, realistic possibility, and gamble. It requires setting *goals* for ourselves and for our relationships. It asks for dreaming and planning. It forces us purposefully to stretch ourselves. Some of our goals may be just around the corner, for today or tomorrow; some may be lifelong. Some may be small, others grand. Some may be for ourselves alone; others may be dreams for the benefit of many. Purposeful living means to follow the path with heart and to rest when you are weary.

Purposeful living is a process of moving *assertively* in the direction of our goals. We can't live purposefully if we passively follow the dictates of family, society, or culture, or give up our goals and dreams because of family, social, or peer pressure. To live puposefully is not the path of least resistance, or to give up because of hardship, or to bully or diminish others or use them aggressively for our own ends. It is a process of knowing what we want from life and asking for it. In some cases, you may have to insist, to draw a line beyond which you are unwilling to go.

Living a life of purpose means being water. I heard once of a Sumo wrestler who possessed great skills and yet was unsuccessful in the contest. He quit wrestling and devoted himself to meditation and study with a wise and scholarly teacher. One of his lessons was to contemplate the ocean waves. In his contemplation, the wrestler saw the wisdom of the lesson. The waves of the ocean are constant, powerful, and irresistible. No matter what we construct to hold it back, water will find a way through if one exists. The wrestler became like the ocean waves and one of the most renowned champions of Sumo. Assertiveness means having a realistic understanding of the possibilities of success and moving consistently, perhaps relentlessly, in that direction. Know that following a dream is not a gentle undertaking.

Assertiveness should not imply irresponsibility. Purpose carries with it *responsibility*. "Doing your own thing" is a fine philosophy

145

as long as you live in a society of one, but no one of us does—hermits notwithstanding. Therefore, our behavior is limited by respect for the goals and purposes of others. Responsibility means that as we move in the direction of our purposes, we do so with regard for others.

Responsibility requires the means to be worthy of the end. If you play sports, you know that any victory is soured by cheating. Competitive sporting events are often the stage on which our ethical and moral lives are portrayed. Whatever flaws of character we may possess are somehow exposed in the intensity of competition. If we follow this analogy, then whatever flaws of character we may have are exposed in our pursuit of our dreams. The role of responsibility is to bridge our flaws of character. Demanding responsible action from ourselves is the preventive for selfishness.

Living with purpose means developing the *competence* to achieve our dreams. It is not a process of wishful thinking in which we hope our dreams will come true. Whatever our dreams or goals, to live with purpose we must develop the skills necessary to ensure that our wishes *can* come true. When asked as a young man why he read so much, Abraham Lincoln is supposed to have said, "I am studying now so that when my time comes I will be ready." The story may be apocryphal, but the advice is sound. Luck happens when opportunity meets preparation. Dreams require preparation.

If we are to move consistently in the direction of our goals, we need *commitment* and perseverance. Some goals may be small and temporary. They come easily and with little effort, and the reward is correspondingly small. Some of our dreams are considerable and demand sacrifice and effort. Some take up space and require us to eliminate from our lives the clutter of other, minor plans—forfeited for the greater dream. Our dreams may require us to work when we are weary, to expend more than we are able to give. A dream requires perspiration, yet because it is our dream, we find the resolve, the time, and the strength to pursue it.

Living with purpose requires *resilience*. Purpose brings the possibility of disappointment, disillusionment, and dejection, but the ability to recover from disappointment permits the ultimate realization of purpose. Resilience forestalls cynicism and pessimism.

The ability to bounce back from setbacks separates the fulfilled person from the discouraged, undernourished one. Resilience also implies a degree of toughness. It suggests the purposeful use of knowledge, skill, and strength in demanding situations when these are needed. Conversely, it may require assertively refusing help when help is not needed, as you insist to family and friends that you must complete the task on your own. The successful completion of some solitary tasks can strengthen our resolve and amplify our resilience.

Living with purpose requires *creativity*. Even the most ordinary goals of life are sometimes not responsive to standard solutions. When this happens, the rigid application of uniform strategies is condemned to failure. Sooner or later, the unexceptional fails when confronted by the extraordinary. Our long-term, complex dreams demand even more of our capacity for flexibility and change. If one way is blocked, another must be found. Creativity is imagination, fancy, whimsy, resourcefulness, and ingenuity. To be creative means that attitudinally we never run out of alternatives. Understand that creativity may alter the very dream itself, as one goal transforms into another. Creative thinking may reveal goals that are equally or even more satisfying. Serendipity plays a role in life, and flexibility permits us to profit from it. Creativity is the ability to turn chance into purpose. The good in good fortune comes from our recognition of its usefulness in our lives. The rigid pursuit of goals, the driven preoccupation with a single end, is not purposeful living. Purposeful living demands that we improvise, alter, and adapt to changing situations and events. Obsession is blind save to its passion. Purposeful living is open, flexible, and adaptive.

No one is separate from others. We are born to one another. We are bound to each other. Each of us is interdependent with the rest. From the most routine act of daily life to our survival as a species we are connected to one another. Turn on a water tap, flip on a light switch, and at the end of a continuous chain of interdependence stands an unknown ally. *Involvement with people* is an aspect of purposeful living. Much is made of our alienation from one another in modern society and I do not wish to dispute that we could be kinder and more caring toward one another. Still, it is wrong to assume that ours is an uncaring society. I live in a moun-

147

tainous state where people sometimes become lost or injured in
the rough terrain. When this happens, a remarkable body of agencies and untold numbers of individuals converge in search-and-res-
cue efforts. Strangers risk their lives. Although it may be their job,
somewhere there is a belief in and a commitment to compassion,
altruism, and service to humanity. Whatever solitary path we walk,
we do not walk it without support. This is the difference between
being alone and being lonely. When we are involved with people,
our tasks may be exclusive but we need not be lonely.

What we desire for ourselves we must permit to others. To live
with purpose and the values it suggests invites a *democratic character structure*. What dream is worth the dehumanization, exploitation, and ruin of another? I heard Barbara Bush, former first lady
of the United States, give a commencement speech in which she
reminded the graduates that the goals we pursue must be chosen
with care. She nudged us with the thought that at life's end we
don't plague ourselves with musing about how life would have been
if we had just spent a little more time at the office, just made one
more sale, driven a Cadillac instead of a Lincoln. What we review is
whether we did right by our children, whether our decisions unnec-
essarily hurt others, whether we were of some use in the world. We
contribute little to raising healthy children, consistently deciding
in favor of people, or contributing much to the world if we do not
respect people. Our human history is teeming with scoundrels and
zealots, lunatics, and monsters whose contribution to humanity
has been damaged lives, ravaged communities, and dysfunctional
societies that responsible and caring people have had to spend their
lives repairing. Democratic character structure permits us to move
in the direction of our dreams as we give to others what we want for
ourselves.

What is the outcome of living with purpose? It is meaning.
Meaning doesn't come with birth. There is seemingly no particular
meaning in the physical universe. The earth spins, it rotates around
the sun; the tides ebb and flow, but the universe is apparently doing nothing and going nowhere. Purpose comes through experience, knowledge, and from the choices and decisions we make in
life. There is great latitude in living and while it is obvious that

some have greater sovereignty than others, many of us can have a voice in deciding our path. It is likely that by the decisions we make and the dreams we pursue that we create our worth in the world. I do not mean worth to others. I mean worth to ourselves. This is not an objective assessment but an internal life review that falls on one side of the line or the other—yes or no. "My life is worthwhile; the costs are not too high; the fare is not too steep; it is worth the trip;"…or not. Meaning is an artifact of purposeful living. It is an epiphenomenon of the decisions we make and the goals we pursue.

One of the troubling myths of life is that many people search for meaning before they believe they can act decisively. They are rendered passive by their confusion. Meaning comes once we have set our goals, practiced strategies that respect our dreams, and moved flexibly in the direction of our dreams. Purpose, the striving for its attainment and the methods of striving, bring significance to life.

Nowhere is purpose more important than in psychotherapy. Many people ask how long psychotherapy will take. The answer is, of course, unknowable. Even in a time when such emphasis is placed on brief therapies (perhaps driven more by economic than therapeutic concerns), no one, psychotherapist or client, knows with certainty the duration of exploration, understanding, and resolution. To predetermine the duration of psychotherapy is artificial and arbitrary. Some psychotherapy is brief because the issues are clear and quickly resolved. Some psychotherapy is long because the problems are vague, even illusive.

149

I live close to the majestic Rocky Mountains. When we hike and come across a stream, we can't always predict how long it will take us to cross it. If we can feel the earth firm beneath our feet and the opposite bank is only a short jump away, we might be able to take it in a single bound. But wider streams take some consideration. We have to somehow determine how deep they are and how fast their current is. The far bank may be rocky or muddy, and the unseen bed of the stream may be treacherous. Then we have to be slow and cautious. I and you know this is a simple analogy, but it serves our purpose here. How much more unpredictable is the human endeavor than crossing a mountain stream. Time can be a thief. It may rob us of the care we need to give to the human predicament. In psychotherapy, one of our fundamental ethical principles is the welfare of the client. The duration of psychotherapy and our intervention should be long enough that clients can leave with a firm sense of their ability to cope with their lives. With anything less, we have not met our responsibilities.

Another answer might well be a riddle. If it took you forty years to become the way you are now, how long will it take to become someone different? People who come to psychotherapy are not fond of riddles. I don't know how long psychotherapy will take, but I do know that it doesn't take forty years. What has occurred through the passage of time, directed by circumstance and unguided process, can be changed. I also believe that what has taken years to happen by chance can be changed in a much shorter time when guided by purpose. I don't know how many years it required to create the Grand Canyon, but it was undoubtedly millions upon millions of years as erosion carved away at resentful rock. The Panama Canal was constructed in less than a decade. I recognize the dangers inherent in comparing geological and physical events with psychological phenomena. My point is that many human issues, problems, and dilemmas that have occurred over time by chance can be amended much more quickly by purpose. Coping with lifelong anxiety can be accomplished in less than a lifetime. We can address life-altering events without merely hoping that time will ease the pain. I don't know whether time heals. I do know that time and purpose together stand a greater chance.

150

24

Becoming a Healer to the Self

*P*ray to God, but continue to swim toward shore. Whether one reads this proverb literally or metaphorically, its message reminds us that we need to take care of ourselves. Taking care of ourselves does not mean giving up hope that others will care about us. It means, however, that we cannot be dependent totally, even minimally, on others. This, of course, is not so for children. For adults, the test of maturity is the willingness and ability to take responsibility for ourselves. We can't always control what happens to us. Situations, events, the behavior of others, often lie outside our control. We cannot be responsible for the turn of the universe. We can, however, be responsible for our own actions, and we can be responsible for our reactions to the situations, events, and the behavior of others. As adults, we have control over our own emotions.

My bedrock wish is that there were no need for psychotherapy. Because I have personally witnessed the good it can do, I am glad we have it. I have participated in the saving of lives literally and figuratively. I have seen the frightened conquer their fears, the tormented overthrow their torments, the timid heart assert itself and look its doubts in the eye. I have seen the depressed churn their way out of the depths of their despair. I have not been a mere observer. I have struggled and persevered with them because psychotherapy is not an antiseptic task. Still, the aim of any psychotherapist is to reach a place with every person who comes for help that he or she feels no further need of assistance. Psychotherapy is not meant to be a lifelong process. Athough no one can predict the length of time or number of sessions psychotherapy will require, I can say without fear of contradiction that the hoped-for outcome or goal is for people to leave psychotherapy more able to cope with life's offerings on their own than when they came.

I am not suggesting that a person reject the help of others. I am not suggesting that we are isolates in the world. I am not suggesting that others cannot be trusted to care about us. I don't believe any of that. I certainly am not suggesting that we remain in a state of *dependence*. I am not even suggesting that we strive for *independence*. One of the damaging myths of life is that our decision is limited to either dependence or independence. The lie in dependence is that we must, since we cannot care for ourselves, wholly depend upon others. The lie in independence is that we can wholly care for ourselves and do not have to depend upon others. Both are untrue. What is closer to a more workable truth is that we are sometimes dependent on others and sometimes autonomous of others. To be interdependent means that we can accept the help of others when we need it and turn down that help when we do not need it. Also, we can offer our help to another when that person needs assistance. That is *interdependence*.

Self-therapy means for the formerly dependent that they are now willing to contend with the difficult and act to overcome the unforeseen. Using self-therapy, they can say to the sources of unnecessary help who have been *caring for* them, that now, in this particular instance, they do not need help. They are willing to look to their own inner resources to cope with the issues that emerge in their lives. They are able to endure and live through troublesome situations and events. They are able to trust their own counsel. Self-therapy implies self-belief, self-trust, self-love. It implies an internal sense of self-competence. Earl Kelly, an educator, called this "a sense of canness," the internal conviction that "I can do what is necessary."[1] In the face of life's upheavals, I can survive and even prosper. Self-therapy means that I can rely on myself as an ally rather than an adversary. I do not have to fear subversion in any struggles to maintain my essential being. Freed from self-destructiveness, I can focus energy on the issues themselves. I can care about me without guilt or selfishness.

Self-therapy does not mean that we give up *caring about* others. One problem that people bring to psychotherapy is that they can easily feel responsible for others. This is a characteristic of both men and women and has little to do with motherhood, female instinct, male dominance, or any of the other political, pop psychology explanations each of us has encountered. Consider what might underlie a strong willingness to take responsibility for others. So long as I am able to take responsibility for others, even if it demands great personal self-sacrifice, I can see myself as strong and be viewed by others as strong. When a person becomes self-therapeutic, caring for others does not disappear. In fact, it might become more effective. What does change is the attitude with which it is given. It becomes *caring about* rather than *caring for* others. Just as self-therapeutic people have moved from the false goals of *dependence* and *independence,* they are now able to discern when help is needed and when it is not. During those times when help is not needed by others, they are able to let others use their own developing strengths. To help when help is not needed is a strategy for developing dependence. When help is needed, they are able to give it freely. When help is needed and withheld is also a strategy for developing dependence. What develops self-therapy in others, what increases personal emotional strength, is allowing others to cope with their own lives when they have a reasonable chance of success and helping when the odds of success are unlikely. Freed from dependence and independence, a self-therapeutic person can choose to be supportive or to actively help another.

What happens, however, when you need something from someone else? You may fear that you are not strong enough to deal with the problem alone. Then you may see this as weakness in yourself. One outcome of psychotherapy can be learning that the people who love you should be allowed to demonstrate their love. Self-therapeutic people are able to recognize those situations and events in which the odds of their success are poor, and they seek the help they need to improve the odds. Just as they care about others and can offer help when it is needed, they can care about themselves and seek help when they need it.

There is a story of a man whose house was flooded. He climbed to the top of the house to avoid the floodwaters. A group of people in a motorboat came by and told him that the waters were rising and that he should come with them. The man said, "No, the Lord will protect me." Later, a man in a rowboat came by and the boatman said, "I have plenty of room. Come with me." The man said, "No, the Lord will protect me." The waters continued to rise and were lapping at the shingles of the roof. At last, a helicopter appeared; the pilot lowered a ladder, and encouraged the man to climb up. But he refused and shouted, "No, the Lord will protect me." The floodwaters continued to rise until they swallowed up the man and he drowned. In heaven, he appeared before the Lord with anger in his heart. He said, "Lord, how could you have failed me? I had such faith. I believed you would protect me and you let me die." And the Lord said, "Well, my goodness! I can't do everything for you. I sent you two boats and a helicopter and you wouldn't take any of them."

To live in the world and believe that we are self-sufficient—that we do not have to rely on the support of others some of the time—is stupid. Accepting help when it is genuinely needed is not dependency or weakness. The ability to give and take makes a self-therapeutic person a real partner in a true relationship.

And so to the end. The goal is to become a self-therapeutic person. Perhaps the ultimate and best lesson of psychotherapy is that we have the stuff to cope with and continually recreate our lives.

Afterword:
The Path of Psychotherapy

To enter the Path of Psychotherapy is to begin together a special relationship. In this relationship, I will do my best to understand who you are. I will do my best to be who I am. I will not judge
you or try to control your life. I will not tell you what to do. I cannot
make you grow or do your growing for you. I will help you to become more aware, more loving, more able to fashion a richer, fuller
life for which you accept responsibility. I cannot protect you from
the pain and suffering of life. On the Path of Psychotherapy, pain
will be part of the experience we share. I will help you to face it,
accept it, and use it to grow. I will be present. I will not hide from
you, even when I am afraid. I will be with you as long as I see you
are, in the smallest way, trying to grow. I will not journey with you
to help you become what is called a normal, adjusted, self-satisfied
person. Nor will I help you to whine and wallow in the misery of
your life. I will help you to take charge of your life and reinvent it. I
will invite you to tell your story as honestly and truly as you are
capable of telling it. I may tell you part of my story when it is appropriate and helpful to do so. I will say hello to you as honestly as I
know how, but my commitment is to encounter you in such a way
that you will decide to say good-bye. I will help you die. I will help
you let go of outgrown and worn-out ways of being so you can be
renewed. It may be painful and terrifying to let go of the old you. I
will not run away from the experience. I believe there is something
in this world here, now, in each of us, a restlessness, a trembling of
something that will not lie in stillness, that seeks renewal, that

seeks to bring us together in responsible love, that invites us to grow and become. We can deny this human spirit. We can deny its expression and be miserable. We can encounter one another in such a way that we will honor it by freeing one another to grow and to be.[1]

156

Endnotes

～

Chapter 2

[1]Morris L. West. (1963). *Shoes of the fisherman.* New York: Morrow.

[2]Brother Blue (Hugh Hill). (1972, Fall). "Miss Wunderlich." *Colorado Journal of Education Research.* 33-34.

Chapter 4

[1]Abraham Maslow. (1970). *Motivation and personality.* New York: Harper and Row.

Chapter 6

[1]*Teenage Mutant Ninja Turtles.* (1990).

Chapter 7

[1]Carl R. Rogers. (1961). *On becoming a person: A therapist's view of psychotherapy.* Boston: Houghton Mifflin.

Chapter 8

[1]From a speech entitled, "Caring for/Caring about" given in 1971 by the psychotheraptist in private practice, Fred Richards, Ph.D., 309 Tanner Street, Carrollton, Georgia 30117.

Chapter 10

[1]From the original television series, *Star Trek,* in the episode "The Empath" (1969).

Chapter 12

[1]Thomas Maeder. (January 1989). "Wounded Healers." *Atlantic Monthly,* 37-47.

[2]Maeder, 38

[3]Ernest Hemingway, (1929,1988). *A farewell to arms.* New York: Macmillan.

[4]Maeder, 40.

Chapter 13

[1]Lynn Hoffman, from a brochure adverstising a conference on psychotherapy.

[2]Personal communication. (1965).

[3]Ken Kesey. (1962). *One flew over the cuckoo's nest.* New York: Viking Press.

Chapter 14

[1]For a readable and informative biography of Anton Mesmer, see F. A. Pattie (1994). *Mesmer and animal magnetism.* Hamilton, NY: Edmonston Publications.

Chapter 16

[1]Personal communication. (1996).

Chapter 18

[1]Jean Paul Satre. (1955). *No exit and other plays.* New York: Vintage Books.

Chapter 21

[1]Max Ehrmann. (b.1872-d.1945). Ehrmann's plan for living is contained in *Disiderata*, written in 1927. You may find *Desiderata* on a wall poster published by Athena International Ltd., London (1991). Or, you may find it as well on the world wide web by using a search engine such as *Lycos* or *Yahoo* and searching for Max Ehrmann.

Chapter 24

[1]Earl Kelly. (1962). *In defense of youth.* Englewood Cliffs, NJ: Prentice-Hall.

Afterword

[1]From a speech given in 1995 by Fred Richards, Ph.D., a psychotherapist in private practice, 309 Tanner Street, Carrollton, GA 30117.

For Further Reading

For each chapter, I have identified selected readings that either informed my writing or that I simply believe will be helpful to the reader who wishes to know more about the topic of that chapter. Some references are books and obviously provide more information than contained in the single chapter for which they are recommended. All I think are helpful and informative.

Chapter 1: The Way We Are

Slater, Philip E. (1970). *The pursuit of loneliness: American culture at the breaking point*. Boston: Beacon Press.

Slater, Philip E. (1974). *Earthwalk*. Garden City, NJ: Anchor Press.

Chapter 2: The Best We Have

Combs, Arthur W. (1989). *A theory of therapy*. Thousand Oaks, CA: Sage.

Combs, Arthur W., & Gonzalez, David M. (1994). *Helping relationships*. Boston, MA: Allyn & Bacon.

Hill, Hugh (Brother Blue). (1972). Miss Wunderlich. *Colorado Journal of Educational Research, 12,* 33–34.

Patterson, C. H. (1984, Winter). Empathy, warmth, and genuineness in psychotherapy: A review of reviews. *Psychotherapy, 21,* 431–438.

Rogers, Carl R. (1957). The necessary and sufficient conditions of therapeutic personality change. *Journal of Consulting Psychology, 21,* 95–103.

Rogers, Carl R. (1961). *On becoming a person: A therapist's view of psychotherapy*. Boston: Houghton Mifflin.

Sexton, Thomas L., & Whiston, Susan C. (1991, June). A review of the empirical basis for counseling: Implications for practice and training. *Counselor Education and Supervision, 30,* 330–354.

West, Morris L. (1963). *Shoes of the fisherman.* New York: Morrow.

Chapter 3: Coping Versus Curing

Bart, Pauline B., & Geil Moran, Eileen (Eds.). (1993). *Violence against women: The bloody footprints. A gender and society reader.* Newbury Park, CA: Sage. (See the chapter by Carole Warshaw, "Limitations of the Medical Model in the Care of Battered Women.")

Dryden, Windy, & Feltham, Colin (Eds.). (1992). *Psychotherapy and its discontents.* Buckingham, England: Open University Press.

Follette, William C., Houts, Arthur C., & Hayes, Steven C. (1992, Fall–Winter). Behavior therapy and the new medical model. *Behavioral Assessment, 14,* 323–343.

Ivey, Allen E. (1990, May–June). Counseling and development: "No one can do it all, but it all needs to be done." *Journal of Counseling and Development, 68,* 534–536.

Lindsman, Moshe S. (1994, December). Needed: Metaphors for the prevention model of mental health. *American Psychologist, 49,* 1086–1087.

Mohr, David C. (1995, Summer). The role of proscription in psychotherapy. *Psychotherapy, 32,* 187–193.

Rave, Elizabeth J., & Larsen, Carolyn C. (Eds.). (1995). *Ethical decision making in therapy.* New York: Guilford Press. (See the chapter by Rosemary Liburd and Ester Rothblum, "The Medical Model.")

Sanua, Victor D. (1994, Spring). Quo vadis APA? Inroads of the medical model. *Humanistic Psychologist, 22,* 3–27.

Simon, Laurence R. (1994). *Psycho "therapy": Theory, practice, modern and postmodern influences.* Westport, CT: Praeger.

Spira, James L., & Yalom, Irvin D. (Eds.). (1996). *Treating dissociative identity disorder.* San Francisco, CA: Jossey-Bass. (See the chapter by Catherine G. Fine, "Models of Helping: The Role of Responsibility.")

Svensson, Tommy. (1995). *On the notion of mental illness: Problematizing the medical-model conception of certain abnormal behaviour and mental afflictions.* Aldershot, England: Avebury/Ashgate.

Waters, David Brooks, & Lawrence, Edith C. (1993). *Competence, courage, and change: An approach to family therapy.* New York: W. W. Norton.

Chapter 4: The Source of the Hurt

Jacobs, David H. (1994, Winter–Spring). Environmental failure: Oppression is the only cause of psychopathology. *Journal of Mind and Behavior, 15,* 1–18.

Kessler, Marc, & Goldsten, Stephen E. (Eds.). (1975). *A decade of progress in prevention.* Hanover, NH: University Press of New England. (See the chapter by Bruce P. Dohrenwend, "Social Stress and Psychopathology.")

Rende, Richard, & Plomin, Robert. (1992, Fall). Diathesis-stress models of psychopathology: A quantitative genetic perspective. *Applied and Preventive Psychology, 1,* 177–182.

Simek-Downing, Lynn (Ed.). (1989). *International psychotherapy: Theories, research and cross-cultural implications.* New York: Praeger. (See the chapter by Mark H. Bickhard, "The Nature of Psychopathology.")

Chapter 5: On Change

Beitman, B. D. (1987). *The structure of individual psychotherapy.* New York: Guilford Press.

Connor-Greene, Patricia A. (1993, Fall). The therapeutic context: Preconditions for change in psychotherapy. *Psychotherapy, 30,* 375–382.

Curtis, Rebecca C., & Stricker, George (Eds.). (1991). *How people change: Inside and outside therapy.* New York: Plenum Press. (See the chapter by Marvin R. Goldfried, "Transtheoretical Ingredients in Therapeutic Change.")

Hanna, Fred J., & Ritchie, Martin H. (1995, April). Seeking the active ingredients of psychotherapeutic change: Within and outside the context of therapy. *Professional Psychology: Research and Practice, 26,* 176–183.

McConnaughy, E. A., DiClemente, C. C., Prochaska, J. O., & Velicer, W. F. (1989). Stages of change in psychotherapy: A follow-up report. *Psychotherapy, 26,* 494–503.

McConnaughy, E. A., Prochaska, J. O., & Velicer, W. F. (1983). Stages of change in psychotherapy: Measurement and sample profiles. *Psychotherapy: Theory, Research, and Practice, 20,* 368–375.

Mishara, Aaron L. (1995, Spring). Narrative and psychotherapy: The phenomenology of healing. *American Journal of Psychotherapy, 49,* 180–195.

Safran, Jeremy D. (Ed.). (1991). *Emotion, psychotherapy, and change.* New York: Guilford Press.

Steenbarger, B. N. (1992). Toward science-practice integration in brief counseling and therapy. *The Counseling Psychologist, 20,* 403–450.

Strong, S. R., & Claiborn, C. D. (1982). *Change through integration.* New York: Wiley.

Suler, John R. (1991, March). The T'ai Chi images: A Taoist model of psychotherapeutic change. *Psychologia: An International Journal of Psychology in the Orient, 34,* 18–27.

Tracey, T. J., & Ray, P. B. (1984). The stages of successful time-limited counseling: An interactional examination. *Journal of Counseling Psychology, 31,* 13–27.

Waters, David Brooks, & Lawrence, Edith C. (1993). *Competence, courage, and change: An approach to family therapy*. New York: W. W. Norton.

Zastrow, Charles. (1988, Spring). What really causes psychotherapy change? *Journal of Independent Social Work, 23,* 5–16.

Chapter 6: On Listening

Havens, Leston. (1986). *Making contact: Uses of language in psychotherapy*. Cambridge, MA: Harvard University Press.

Eckstein, Rudolf. (1989). *The language of psychotherapy*. Amsterdam, Netherlands: John Benjamins.

Hoshmand, Lisa Tsoi, & Martin, Jack (Eds.). (1995). *Research as praxis: Lessons from programmatic research in therapeutic psychology*. New York: Teachers College Press.

Ingram, Joyce L. (1994). The role of figurative language in psychotherapy: A methodological examination. *Metaphor and Symbolic Activity, 9,* 271–288.

Russell, Robert L. (1989). Language and psychotherapy. *Clinical Psychology Review, 9,* 505–519.

Siegelman, Ellen Y. (1990). *Metaphor and meaning in psychotherapy*. New York: Guilford Press.

Chapter 7: On Courage

Boyd, Jon, & Ross, Kate. (1994, Spring). The courage tapes: A positive approach to life's challenges. *Journal of Systemic Therapies, 13,* 64–69.

Edelstein, E. L., Nathanson, Donald L., & Stone, Andrew M. (Eds.). (1989). *Denial: A clarification of concepts and research*. New York: Plenum Press.

Feinstein, Sherman C., Esman, Aaron H., Looney, John G., Schwartzberg, Allan Z., Sorosky, Arthur D., & Sugar, Max (Eds.). (1986). *Adolescent psychiatry: Developmental and clinical studies,* Vol. 13, *Annals of the American Society for Adolescent Psychiatry*. (See the chapter by Herman Sinaiko, "Plato's 'Laches': Courage, Expertise, Psychotherapy, and Adolescence.")

Goldberg, Carl. (1982, Fall–Winter). Toward a psychology of courage: Implications for the change (healing) process. *Journal of Contemporary Psychotherapy, 13,* 107–128.

Kaminer, Wendy. (1993). *I'm dysfunctional, you're dysfunctional: The recovery movement and other self-help fashions*. New York: Vintage Books.

Prince, Robert M. (1984, Spring). Courage and masochism in psychotherapy. *Psychoanalytic Review, 71,* 47–61.

Waters, David Brooks, & Lawrence, Edith C. (1993). *Competence, courage and change: An approach to family therapy*. New York: W. W. Norton.

Chapter 8: On Caring

DeMarinis, Valerie M. (1993). *Critical caring: A feminist model for pastoral psychology*. Louisville, KY: Westminster/John Knox Press.

Larson, Dale G. (1993). *The helper's journey: Working with people facing grief, loss and life-threatening illness*. Champaign, IL: Research Press.

Mayeroff, Milton. (1971). *On caring*. New York: Harper & Row.

Richards, Fred, & Richards, Anne C. (1973). *Homonovus: The new man*. Boulder, CO: Shields.

Chapter 9: On Being Tough and Tender

Hoffman, John C. (1979). *Ethical confrontation in counseling*. Chicago: University of Chicago Press.

Mehlman, Elizabeth, & Glickauf-Hughes, Cheryl. (1994, Fall). The underside of psychotherapy: Confronting hateful feelings toward clients. *Psychotherapy, 31*, 434–439.

Nevins, Bradley G. (1989). *Confrontive interventions in psychotherapy*. Los Angeles: California School of Professional Psychology. (For a summary, see *Dissertation Abstracts International, 50*, 1652, October 1989.)

Chapter 10: On Being Close; On Being Separate

Connor-Greene, Patricia A. (1993, Fall). The therapeutic context: Preconditions for change in psychotherapy. *Psychotherapy, 30*, 375–382. (See the section on therapeutic alliance).

Neimeyer, Robert A., & Mahoney, Michael J. (Eds.). (1995). *Constructivism in psychotherapy*. Washington, DC: American Psychological Association. (See the chapter by Larry M. Leitner, "Optimal Therapeutic Distance: A Therapist's Experience of Personal Construct Psychotherapy.")

Safran, Jeremy D. (1993, Spring). Breaches in the therapeutic alliance: An arena for negotiating authentic relatedness. *Psychotherapy, 30*, 11–24.

Schwartz, Richard S. (1993, Winter). Managing closeness in psychotherapy. *Psychotherapy, 30*, 601–607.

Chapter 11: What the Mind Can Imagine

Bellack, Alan S., & Hersen, Michel. (1985). *Dictionary of behavior therapy techniques*. New York: Pergamon Press.

Dyer, Wayne W., & Vriend, John. (1977). *Counseling techniques that work*. New York: Funk and Wagnalls.

Johnson, David R. (1991). *The arts in psychotherapy*. Arts in Psychotherapy, *18*, 285–300.

Kanfer, Frederick H., & Goldstein, Arnold P. (1986). *Helping people change: A textbook of methods*. New York: Pergamon Press.

Karasu, Toksoz B., & Bellack, Leopold. (1980). *Specialized techniques in individual psychotherapy*. New York: Brunnel/Mazel.

Mozdziertz, Gerald J., & Greenblatt, Richard L. (1994, June). Technique in psychotherapy: Cautions and concerns. *Individual Psychology: Journal of Adlerian Theory, Research and Practice, 50*, 232–249.

Siegelman, Ellen Y. (1990). *Metaphor and meaning in psychotherapy*. New York: Guilford Press.

Vriend, John. (1985). *More counseling techniques that work*. Alexandria, VA: Association for Supervision and Development.

Chapter 12: Wounded Healers

Allen, Margaret R. (1989). *Wounded healers: Alleviation of burnout in psychotherapists through integration of altruistic and self-healing motivations*. Berkeley: California School of Professional Psychology. (For a summary, see *Dissertation Abstracts International, 50*, 1144, September 1989.)

Bernard, Michael E. (Ed). (1991). *Using rational-emotive therapy: a practitioner's guide*. New York: Plenum Press. (See the chapter by Susan R. Walen and Mary W. Rader, "Depression and RET: Perspectives from Wounded Healers.")

Goldwert, Marvin. (1992). *The wounded healers: Creative illness in the pioneers of depth psychology*. Lanham, MD: University Press of America.

Grapp, Pamela R. (1993). *Wounded healers: An exploratory study of therapist early trauma, career development and self-disclosure*. Eugene: University of Oregon. (For a summary, see *Dissertation Abstracts International, 53*, 5434. April 1993.)

Maeder, Thomas. (1989, January). Wounded healers. *Atlantic Monthly*, pp. 37–47.

Muse, Steven, & Chase, Edwin. (1993, Summer). Healing the wounded healers: "Soul" food for clergy. *Journal of Psychology and Christianity, 12*, 141–150.

Chapter 13: The Problem of Power

Alinsky, Saul D. (1989). *Rules for radicals: A practical primer for realistic radicals*. New York: Vintage. (Original work published 1971)

Alinsky, Saul D. (1989). *Reveille for radicals*. New York: Vintage. (Original work published 1969)

Burck, Charlotte, & Bebe, Speed. (1995). *Gender, power, and relationships*. New York: Routledge.

Guggenbuhl-Craig, Adolf. (1989). *Power in the helping professions*. Dallas, TX: Spring Publications. (Original work published 1971)

May, Rollo. (1972). *Power and innocence: A search for the sources of violence*. New York: W. W. Norton.

Rinella, Vincent J., & Gerstein, Alvin I. (1994, Summer). The development of dual relationships: Power and professional responsibility. *International Journal of Law and Psychiatry, 17*, 225–237.

Rogers, Carl R. (1977). *On personal power*. New York: Delacorte Press.

Tirnauer, Lawrence. (1985, Summer). Power and terror of change. *Psychotherapy Patient, 1*, 33–38.

Vincent, Nan. (1987, July). Psychotherapy as an Easter egg hunt: A modest proposal on power. *Transactional Analysis Journal, 17*, 99–101.

Chapter 14: On Pundits, Wizards, Priests, and Clerks

Pattie, F. A. (1994). *Mesmer and animal magnetism*. Hamilton, NY: Edmonston Publishing.

Chapter 16: The Ethics of Psychotherapy

Corey, Gerald, Corey, Marianne, & Callanan, Patrick. (1993). *Issues and ethics in the helping professions*. Pacific Grove, CA: Brooks/Cole.

Lerman, Hannah, & Porter, Natalie. (1990). *Feminist ethics in psychotherapy*. New York: Spring.

Schulte, John M. (1995). *Ethics in school counseling*. New York: Teachers College Press.

Chapter 17: Paths of Diversity

Chin, Jean L., & De La Cancela, Victor. (1993). *Diversity in counseling: The politics of race, ethnicity and gender*. Westport, CT: Praeger.

Paul B. Pederson. (1996). *Counseling across cultures*. Thousands Oaks, CA: Sage.

Ponterotto, Joseph C., Casas, J. Manual, Suzuki, Lisa A., & Alexander, Charlene M. (Eds.). (1995). *Handbook of multicultural counseling*. Thousands Oaks, CA: Sage.

Sue, Derald Wing, & Sue, Donald. (1990). *Counseling the culturally different: Theory and practice*. New York: Wiley.

Chapter 18: Issues, Problems, and Dilemmas

Doka, Kenneth J. (1996). *Living with grief after sudden loss: Suicide, homicide, accident, heart attack, stroke.* Hospice Foundation of America. Bristol, PA: Taylor and Francis.

Kushner, Harold S.. (1982). *When bad things happen to good people.* Boston, MA: G. K. Hall.

Perls, Frederick S. (1969). *In and out of the garbage pail.* Lafayette, CA: Real People Press.

Marris, Peter. (1975). *Loss and change: What happens to us when we divorce, lose a loved one, change our job or business, move, or simply try to deal with the change in our everyday lives.* Garden City, NJ: Anchor Books.

Chapter 19: Your Past Is Not Your Potential

Bugental, James F. T. (1987). *The art of the psychotherapist.* New York: W. W. Norton.

Friedman, Steven (Ed.). (1993). *The new language of change: Constructive collaboration in psychotherapy.* New York: Guilford Press.

Rodman, F. Robert. (1986). *Keeping hope alive: On becoming a psychotherapist.* New York: Harper & Row.

Rumsfeld, Valerie. (1991). *The dance of hope: An inquiry into the psychological nature and function of hope.* Boston: Massachusetts School of Professional Psychology.

Chapter 20: Choices Versus Decisions

Headlee, Raymond, & Kalogjera, Ikar J. (1988, October). The psychopathology of choice. *American Journal of Psychotherapy, 42,* 532–542.

Chapter 21: On Perfection

Field, Nathan. (1992, Winter). The way of imperfection. *British Journal of Psychotherapy, 9,* 139–147.

Kottler, Jeffery A., & Blau, Diane S. (1989). *The imperfect therapist: Learning from failure in therapeutic practice.* San Francisco, CA: Jossey-Bass.

Strube, Michael J. (1991). *Type A behavior.* Newbury Park, CA: Sage Publications.

Chapter 22: Die Gedanken Sind Frei (Thoughts Are Free)

Green, Daniel R., & Lawrenz, Mel. (1994). *Encountering shame and guilt: a short-term structured model.* Grand Rapids, MI: Baker Books.

Tangney, June Price. (1995, August). Recent advances in the empirical study of shame and guilt. *American Behavioral Scientist, 38,* 1132–1145.

Tangney, June Price, & Fischer, Kurt W. (Eds.). (1995). *Self-conscious emotions: The psychology of shame, guilt, embarrassment, and pride.* New York: Guilford Press.

Chapter 23: Living with Purpose

Coan, Richard W. (1977). *Hero, artist, sage or saint? A survey of views on what is variously called mental health, normality, maturity, self-actualization, and human fulfillment.* New York: Columbia University Press.

Eigen, Michael. (1995). *Reshaping the self: Reflections on renewal through therapy.* Madison, CT: Psychosocial Press.

Goldman, Daniel, & Gurin, Joel. (1993). *Mind, body and medicine: How to use your mind for better health.* Yonkers, NY: Consumer Report Books.

Hermans, H. J. M. (1995). *Self-narration: The construction of meaning in psychotherapy.* New York: Guilford Press.

Jourard, Sidney M., & Landsman, Ted. (1980). *Healthy personality: An approach from the viewpoint of humanistic psychology* (4th Ed). New York: Macmillan.

Maslow, Abraham H. (1970). *Motivation and personality* (2nd Ed). New York: Harper & Row.

Maslow, Abraham H. (1971). *Further reaches of human nature.* New York: Vintage.

Maslow, Abraham H. (1987). *Motivation and personality* (3rd Ed). Revised by Robert Frager, James Fadiman, Cynthia McReynolds, & Ruth Cox. New York: Harper & Row. (See the section on self-actualization.) (Original work published 1970)

Rogers, Carl R. (1972). *A therapist's view of personal goals.* Pendle Hill Pamphlet No. 108. Wallingford, PA: Pendle Hill.

167

Chapter 24: Becoming a Healer to the Self

Deci, Edward L. (1980). *The psychology of self-determination.* Lexington, MA: D. C. Health.

Jourard, Sidney M. (1971). *The transparent self.* New York: Van Nostrand Reinhold. (Original work published 1964)

Maslow, Abraham H. (1968). *Toward a psychology of being.* Princeton, NJ: Van Nostrand.

Rogers, Carl R. (1961). *On becoming a person: A therapist's view of psychotherapy.* Boston: Houghton Mifflin.

Seligman, Martin E. P. (1991). *Learned optimism.* New York: Knopf.

Index

ᴕ

TO THE OWNER OF THIS BOOK:

I hope that you have found *The Path of Psychotherapy: Matters of the Heart* useful. So that this book can be improved in a future edition, would you take the time to complete this sheet and return it? Thank you.

School and address: —————————————————————————

Department: —————————————————————————

Instructor's name: —————————————————————————

1. What I like most about this book is: —————————————————

—————————————————————————————

—————————————————————————————

2. What I like least about this book is: —————————————————

—————————————————————————————

—————————————————————————————

3. My general reaction to this book is: —————————————————

—————————————————————————————

4. The name of the course in which I used this book is: ————————

—————————————————————————————

5. Were all of the chapters of the book assigned for you to read? ——————

   If not, which ones weren't? ————————————————————

6. In the space below, or on a separate sheet of paper, please write specific suggestions for improving this book and anything else you'd care to share about your experience in using the book.

—————————————————————————————

—————————————————————————————

—————————————————————————————

—————————————————————————————

—————————————————————————————

Optional:

Your name: _____ Date: _____

May Brooks/Cole quote you, either in promotion for *The Path of Psychotherapy: Matters of the Heart* or in future publishing ventures?

Yes: _____ No: _____

Sincerely,

Ira David Welch

FOLD HERE

- -

NO POSTAGE
NECESSARY
IF MAILED
IN THE
UNITED STATES

BUSINESS REPLY MAIL

FIRST CLASS   PERMIT NO. 358   PACIFIC GROVE, CA

POSTAGE WILL BE PAID BY ADDRESSEE

ATT: *Ira David Welch*

Brooks/Cole Publishing Company
511 Forest Lodge Road
Pacific Grove, California 93950-9968

- -

FOLD HERE